Nancy Brophy Romance Author & Killer

Pete Dove

Published by Trellis Publishing, 2021.

While every precaution has been taken in the preparation of this book, the publisher assumes no responsibility for errors or omissions, or for damages resulting from the use of the information contained herein.

NANCY BROPHY ROMANCE AUTHOR & KILLER

First edition. July 11, 2021.

Copyright © 2021 Pete Dove.

ISBN: 979-8224004683

Written by Pete Dove.

NANCY BROPHY, KILLER ROMANCE AUTHOR

1

PETE DOVE

MARY WINKLER
TRACEY GRISSOM
MICHELLE HALL
MICHELLE REYNOLDS

The Puzzle of Fiction Becoming Fact

Where am I?

During the Ice Age, I would be under four hundred feet of freezing glacial waters. Back in the 1830s people would have embarked on a long and dangerous trek across country to reach me. I am pretty big, in fact the twenty-fifth largest in my country and, in my early days, I was known as Stumpsville.

Bit of a mystery? Rightly so. A few more clues might be needed. I am in the Pacific North West, based on a wide and magnificent river, and – here is the killer (pun intended) – my city's guidebook was awarded the best of its kind. In 2014.

Still no closer? Then, look into the distance and a magnificent mountain smiles down on me from afar. I could almost be in a Paramount movie from the 1950s, full of handsome men and romantic themes.

I am, of course, in the wonderful city of Portland, close to the Canadian border in the bountiful state of Oregon. Not the place, most people would assume, for the sort of murder whose mysterious plot and romantic overtones seems right out of the script of a hard to believe fifties' romantic tear jerker, the sort of Saturday afternoon B flick in which Paramount specialized back in the day. Or, for that matter, the pages of an escapist novel from the pen of a little-known writer.

Then again, maybe the latter is a possibility. A much greater possibility than we, or the police, at first realized.

Nancy Crampton-Brophy is not John Grisham or J.K. Rowling or E.L, James. Nor is she Barbara Cartland or, for that matter, Jackie Collins. But she aspires to be as successful as these names from popular literature. No doubt, she would love to see her works on stands in airport bookshops or brightening the plate glass windows of Barnes and Noble. It is with painful irony that her current predicament might lead to a greater chance of her achieving this goal than her words could ever do.

Nancy is not a great writer, at least in terms of the sales of her books. Her words are not discussed on late night TV's more obscure cable channels, the only time intellectualism might knock the kinds of plots found in her books off the main channels of the goggle box. Her characters are not evaluated in national newspapers or the more prestigious book magazines. Her catalogue is unlikely to appear on an exam syllabus. Her output is considerable – in one year she set herself the task of writing a book a month – a goal she almost reached. Quantity over, well, originality her critics might argue.

But Brophy does have her fans. Her Amazon reviews might be few and far between, but those she does get tend to be positive. Admittedly, there is the odd moan about typographic errors, the sort of mistake that a publishing house would spot, but Brophy does not enjoy that luxury (although, if her trial goes the way she wants it to, her unwanted notoriety might spur one or two literary companies to spot the potential for big sales, and send her the kind of letter she has sought for most of her career).

For Nancy Crampton-Brophy is one of that vast and welcome legion of self-publishers, a writer who twenty years ago would simply have a drawer full of rejection letters and a mind full of thwarted ambition. Now she can publish her works herself, and she does so with gusto. Or, more accurately *did* so with gusto. The events of 2018 led to a notable drop off in her creative output. But let us not hurry too quickly to the cliff-hanger. Instead, we'll build context and backstory. There's much to be said for self-publishing. Let's be honest, under the old regime you needed one of a very limited range of benefits to fall your way in order to make any kind of publishing grade.

A literary name helped, or some connection to the industry. Celebrity of another kind helped sales, no doubt about that. Occasionally, if combined with exceptional luck, extreme talent might get you a publishing deal. Take the aforementioned JK Rowling; she certainly knows how to tell a story, but her Harry Potter books are not especially original. She tapped in on the ground set by the likes of Anthony Buckeridge, with his tales of boarding school life in a British Prep School, becoming a sort of Enid Blyton combined with tints of Tolkien. (Note: a Prep School is a British private school in which very small children are dragged out of the arms of their mothers and, certainly during Buckeridge's day, beaten for the various pleasures of their beaks and masters – see British Public School etymology for an explanation of these archaic terms)

The chances are that Brophy, with her penchant for, in her own words 'stories...about pretty men and strong women, about families that don't always work and about the joy of finding love and the difficult of making it stay' would never had seen a story bought up by a publishing house. Advances would for ever stay so advanced that they were out of reach; the drudge of book tours and signings, and giving interviews to people who have never read your book and have not the slightest interest in it would remain no more than a dream.

But self-publishing changed that, for Brophy and for tens of thousands of authors like her. And a good thing too. Niche subjects and topics which would never have found the light of day, unless funded benevolently by the author themselves, no longer go untold. Genuine talent is given a better chance of finding an audience.

Yet there is a downside to self-publishing; it doesn't pay very well. Even for one as (very) moderately successful in the field as Brophy, the chances of making a fortune are slimmer than a size zero model. And that, it seems (to prosecutors at least) was the problem.

For all that, murders are sadly plentiful in the US, even in Oregon and even in a city as pleasant as Portland. Brophy is still awaiting trial, and as we shall see, the evidence against her seems shaky, according to her attorneys. So, she may not be a murderer; she is certainly not a mass murderer. Admittedly, people who kill are rarely professional writers, but even though that makes her unusual, she is hardly (or was, hardly) a household name. Her notoriety is therefore, clearly, down to another reason.

That is that, once upon a time, Nancy Crampton-Brophy wrote an essay. One which has subsequently captured the imaginations of a nation of headline writers and those who enjoy a half decent pun or the concept of an idea coming back to bite its creator.

That essay was published in November 2011, nearly seven years before the death of the husband whose demise she is alleged to have caused (a claim she vehemently denies.) It contains lines such as the following: 'As a romantic suspense writer, I spend a lot of time thinking about murder...After all, if the murder is supposed to set me free, I certainly don't want to spend any time in jail...orange isn't my color.' In the essay, she goes on to say: 'I find it is easier to wish people dead than to actually kill them. But then what I think I know about murder is that every one of us have it in him/her when pushed far enough.'

The title of this piece is, incredibly, now infamous: 'How to Murder Your Husband.' The plot to this potential blockbuster has just taken a twist nobody could have seen coming. Unless, of course, they stayed up to date with Portland news.

Daniel Brophy was a teacher and a chef. He taught cookery at the Oregon Culinary Institute in Portland, where he was chief instructor. Called an 'encyclopedia' by his colleagues, he enjoyed a specialism in, of all things, fungi. When he was killed, in June 2018, he was sixty-three years old, a few years younger than his wife of twenty-seven years, Nancy.

Daniel was a popular teacher. Following his death tributes were paid by colleagues, current and ex-students, as well as Nancy herself. Whether she was keeping up appearances, or genuinely distraught and confused by his murder we can only surmise. Perhaps a card left by a student from the Class of 2013, Neil Larecco, sums up feelings towards the friendly teacher cum cook. 'Chef', it read, 'Thank-you for your Brophy-isms, your instruction, your personal Puttanesca Sauce Recipe.

But most of all your friendship. Bon Appetit, Chef!' A smiley, cheerful hand drawn emoji gave an insight into the way those he had taught wished to remember him.

Nancy, too, seemed as distraught as any unexpectedly grieving widow would be. Too upset to telephone anybody with the terrible news, she sent a message via Facebook to friends and colleagues. "For my Facebook friends and family,' it read, 'I have sad news to relate. My husband and best friend, Chef Dan Brophy was killed yesterday morning. For those of you who are close to me and feel this deserved a phone call, you are right, but I'm struggling to make sense of everything right now. There is a candle-light vigil at Oregon Culinary Institute tomorrow, Monday, June 4th at 7 pm. While I appreciate all of your loving responses, I am overwhelmed. Please save phone calls for a few days until I can function."

At the function, Nancy seemed much as any woman unfortunate enough to find themselves in her position would be. Distracted, bemused but trying to hold it together. Maybe she is an outstanding actress, or perhaps the emotions she seemed to be displaying were genuine. Similarly, eighteen months later at pretrial hearings, she appears to be exactly as confused as any of us might find ourselves in similar circumstances. Looking much older for the stress she has been through, hair untidy and straggly rather than neatly coiffured as before, her poor health and age seems to weigh much heavier upon her. She looks as she probably is – a woman whose life has turned upside down.

Whether this upheaval was the result of her own actions is, of course the problem the court must resolve. Doing so may prove to be difficult.

One of the issues in this case, which the jury will need to see through, is that the writing – fiction and non-fiction - Brophy produced in her professional life seems so closely linked to the crime which took place that the two can become overly intertwined. If she had contented herself with just writing stories, dramatically romanticised ones in which the apparently demure little heroine generally turns out to hold a core of best quality steel, and every hero is a handsome Heathcliff with a heart of hewed gold, then the gap would be easier to discern.

Probably.

Because it cannot be denied that today we live in a world of celebrity, one where the actions of the Kardashians, or the interplay of Prince Harry and Meghan Markle hold far more import that they really should. Where the public, in too many cases, find the lines between fiction, faction and genuine truth so misted that they become one.

It will be even harder in the case of Nancy Crampton-Brophy because she saw herself, vainly or rightly, as more than just an author. Rather, as an expert who could provide lessons and learning for others. Despite having only modest success herself (if that) she produced copious articles and pages offering guidance to would be writers and provided a service whereby she would review extracts of would-be novels and offer feedback. For a fee, of course.

During the course of this work she produced numerous documents which could easily sway a gullible – or perhaps perceptive, depending on the truth – jury member against her.

Let us start with another extract from the essay now so beloved of the lower end of the media market, 'How to Murder Your Husband', which originally appeared on the See Jane website. 'Divorce is expensive, and do you really want to split your possessions?' she demands. Or, in a more philosophical tone she asks of would be domestic killers, 'What if killing didn't produce the right result? Would they do it again? Could they do it again? What if they liked it?'

Another essay produced from the pen of the prolific wordsmith is entitled, 'When Marriage Fails Us'. Here she emotes 'Love is tough. Riding off into the sunset may blind you temporarily, but sooner or later your sight returns. Everyone's story includes pain and underneath it all, we share the same story.'

But then she comes back to the idea that it is important to ride out the inevitable tempests of married life. 'I read somewhere,' she writes, 'that after being divorced for a couple of years, most people believe they could have made it work, if only they'd tried harder.'

Some of Brophy's fiction also errs towards the idea of getting rid of a husband. She published a series of books called 'The Wrong...' (as in, for example, 'The Wrong Cop'). Among this collection is a novel entitled 'The Wrong Husband', where the heroine fakes her own death to escape the clutches of her abusive partner. In 'The Wrong Cop', the protagonist spends, in the writer's own words, 'every day of her marriage fantasising about killing' – the planned victim being her husband.

But surely, jury members will see beyond the obvious conclusion here. Brophy might be a hereto undiscovered literary gem of a writer, or a rather ordinary one whose plots are predictable and story lines familiar and romantically unreal. But there is a difference between fiction and reality. Even when, on the 'about me' page of her website she opines, 'In writing fiction you dig deep and unearth portions of your own life that you've long forgotten or had purposely buried deep. Granted' she adds with either terrible irony or unintended foresight, 'sometimes it is smarter to change the ending.'

Even her more factual writing is just that. Writing. Not necessarily truth. Or intent. Or plans. Just writing. So, when she published the aforementioned article, 'How to Murder Your Husband', or even when she discovered (as prosecutors were please to share) a little known piece entitled 'How to Cover Up a Murder', only the foolish and overly dramatic read too much into it.

Except... It has to be said, the state of Nancy and Daniel's marriage was hard to determine. Certainly, on her website she describes the relationship positively, and with suitable amour. Mostly. 'I can't tell you when I fell in love with my husband,' she relates in best romantic writer mode, 'but I relate the moment I decided to marry him. I was in the bath. It was a big tub. I expected him to join me and when he was delayed, I called out "Are you coming?"'

She goes on to quote his reply. 'Yes, but I'm making hors d'oeuvres.' The response causes her to pose a rhetorical question to her probably small audience. 'Can you imagine spending the rest of your life without a man like that?'

Well, we might conclude, very possible yes. Is that the conscious, or even more worryingly, sub conscious intent of those words? That Daniel is not quite the man she dreamed about; a bit of a disappointment compared to the heroes of her novels? Well, so what if it is? And, actually, is it any of our business? As you can see, the sub plots of this case are myriad and complex. Other references to Daniel are complimentary, but always in a measured, slightly ambiguous way. Perhaps that is surprising for a woman who creates stories around impossibly passionate affairs. Or, then again, perhaps it is not.

In the web page she observes, 'Like all marriages, we've had our ups and downs, more good times than bad.' Earlier, she introduces Daniel to her readers thus: '(I'm) married to a Chef whose mantra is: life is a science project.' She balances this far from hyperbolic endorsement of her husband's character by describing the joy of having a chef for a partner, one who raises his own chickens and grows his own vegetables, before turning these natural resources into a joyful gastronomic celebration each night. One which, she says, bringing her readers back to earth, leaves her into a constant battle with her weight. She ends the paragraph with another far from glorious adulation. 'The old adage is true,' Nancy Crampton-Brophy warns, 'Be careful what you wish for, when the gods are truly angry, they grant us our wishes.'

But we might argue, this is yet another example of Nancy the writer not Nancy the person. We should take the comments with a large pinch of literary salt. Fair enough, but neighbours of the couple also report somewhat guardedly on their relationship.

'They were pretty quiet,' said one neighbor after Nancy's arrest. 'I never really saw them together very often.' Another, Dan McConnell, said that Nancy, following Daniel's death, 'never showed any signs of being upset or sad. I would say she had an air of relief, almost like a godsend.' Others commented that Nancy showed 'no emotion' when she discovered she was a suspect in the murder of her husband.

So, what exactly happened in this weird story, one which is stranger than some fiction (although, perhaps not that from the pen of the alleged perpetrator)? Daniel Brody had left early for work on the morning of June 2nd. We will not read too much into the fact that a 'tip' from the article 'How to Cover Up a Murder' suggested that a killer should strike early in the day.

It is not clear why he left so early to drive to work; perhaps he had a lot of preparation to undertake, perhaps there was a more sinister reason.

He was working in his kitchen, it seems, when his assailant shot him in the back. Then, as he lay dying on the floor, another bullet was pumped into his chest. At about 8.30 am his students and fellow instructors began to arrive. His body was discovered around this time. The call to the emergency services stated: 'The patient is an instructor at the location. He's bleeding out of his chest and his ribs are broken.' But, despite the best efforts of paramedics, he could not be revived and died at the scene.

At the vigil which followed a couple of days later, Nancy said: 'Dan was one of the few people I've ever known who did exactly what he wanted in life and loved doing it.' Although such a statement might seem a tad overly romantic, even sugary, it seems to be the case in Daniel Brophy's case. A student of his, who did not wish to be named, told the local cable news channel: 'He was a friend to everybody in the school, holding things at the weekend to help you learn more.'

Initially, there was nothing to link Nancy to the murder of her husband. Then, according to prosecutors, little nuggets of evidence began to emerge. There was the CCTV footage gathered locally which showed a minivan circulating around near the Institute. It was the same make and colour as the one driven by Nancy Crampton-Brophy. Yet, that in itself is hardly definitive. The minivan in question is a popular model, a Toyota. There are plenty of owners of such a vehicle.

Then there was the letter she asked for from the police to confirm that she was not a suspect in the case. This was for her insurance company, so they could pay out the policy she had taken out on Daniel's life. Suddenly, warning bells began to ring. Whether any fire was real, or a false alarm is a metaphor the court must unravel.

Next came a more decisive breakthrough, although still one heavily disputed by Nancy's defense team. They argue that the evidence against her is so fragile that the entire case should be dropped.

Police worked out that the murder weapon was a Glock pistol. Nancy revealed that, about eighteen months prior to her husband's killing, they had acquired such a weapon at a gun show. However, she argued, it had never been fired.

On her arrest, she told officers, 'You're arresting me? You must think I murdered my husband.' That was indeed the thoughts they were having.

Yet investigations into the weapon proved that it had indeed never been fired. However, police were not prepared to give up easily. They investigated further and claim that her internet search history proved that she had googled 'Ghost Guns', purchased a gun kit online from a website discovered in the search, and bought a slide and barrel on eBay. Later, they argue, she had closed down her eBay account.

The prosecution team in her case allege that she replaced the original slide and barrel from the pistol with the parts she had purchased on line, used the gun to kill her husband and then sold the used items back on eBay after replacing them with the unused originals. The Multnomah County District Attorney, Rod Underhill, argues that doing this enabled her to be 'able to present a new, fully intact firearm to police that would not be a match to the shell casings she left at the scene.'

Plausible enough, perhaps, although the question is begged whether one who had researched sufficiently to use their gun in this way would overlook the likelihood that CCTV would catch her minivan on camera. Particularly as Underhill admitted 'She planned and carried out what she believed was the perfect murder. '

But Underhill seems as guilty as the headline writers in mixing Nancy's professional work with her real life. 'Nancy Brophy once wrote that finances could be motivation for murdering,' he observed in his court filing.

Certainly, Nancy's own attorneys believe that she should not even be held awaiting trial, and that all charges should be dropped forthwith. They argue that the Prosecution case is 'paper thin'. They say that the police's DNA evidence is highly suspect. They point out that there was no DNA on the shell casings left behind from the bullets which killed the teaching chef. They disagree with the police that the gun had ever been fired, and that a crime lab report into the weapon showed that the police had tainted it as a piece of evidence, and as such it was too unreliable to be used against her.

Further, they argue that the police have been wanton in their failure to preserve evidence safely. Perhaps, floats the implicit suggestion, because that evidence is so insubstantial? Maybe, reading between the lines, they believe that the police and DA feel that a case based on the drama of a writer of murder mysteries killing her husband is more likely to succeed with a jury than their dodgy DNA.

The defense team filed a motion, so far unsuccessful, to dismiss the case, in which they argue: 'She (Nancy) asked to hire forensic experts who could test the physical evidence and challenge the weak tea on which the state's case rests. The defense efforts have been frustrated again and an again and again by the state's loss, destruction or failure to preserve key evidence in this case.'

A further reason for pushing for charges to be dropped is a fear that, locked away in a crowded prison, the elderly suspect, who is overweight and suffers from diabetes, is particularly vulnerable to Corona Virus. It would be a tragic irony if she were indeed innocent but fell victim to the fatal disease.

However, police have one more weapon in their mis-firing armoury. Despite the romanticism of Crampton-Brophy's novels, the soap opera pleasure some would find in a woman who wrote an article about killing a husband actually carrying out the deed, this firearm is much more basic. Money.

Because, the Brophy's did not have any. They were heavily in debt. Nancy liked to spend and had ambitions to own more than the small house they occupied in Portland. She wanted to travel the world, to enjoy experiences which would contrast to life as a failing novelist, whose book sales were meagre. She was desperate not to be a writer who had to work as a hair stylist and an insurance broker to make ends meet.

Daniel earned little. Teaching is not the best paid job under any circumstances, but the level at which he taught pays poorly indeed. Yet, while Nancy had ambitions to see the world, to live the life of a successful writer which her book sales did not justify, Daniel was happy and contented with his lot.

This, argue prosecutors, was the reason that Nancy Crampton-Brophy killed her husband. Not only would she get the $1.5 million insurance pay-out from the policy she had taken out – a policy that she ensured was paid up to date even though other bills were left untouched due to their perilous financial state – but her property was worth another $300000. Plenty of money to spend years travelling and writing. The glories of the globe, she may have hoped, inspiring her to find the best seller she longed to produce.

'Dan Brophy was worth about $1.5 million to Nancy Brophy if he was dead,' wrote Rod Underhill in his court filings. 'And he was worth a life of financial hardship if he stayed alive.'

And so, Nancy awaits trial, due to begin in the Autumn. Covid 19 permitting. The reliability of police evidence pertaining. Like in the best novels, ones where the plot is hard to predict, anything could happen in this case. Nancy Crampton-Brophy denies murder. She also writes in her website 'All writers are liars.'

Whether this is another example of her professional work and real life running on different tracks is something we await to discover. What is more certain is that there is a great, potentially tragic, story line here. A thriller which would make both a great novel and a wonderful film.

Maybe that mountain which casts its reflection over Portland will inspire Paramount once again.

16

Murder at the Charisma Ranch

Robert Dorotik was born in 1945, two years before his future wife Jane Marguerite Colvey. It would be 23 years before they would meet and fall in love. They married on April 4, 1970 in Los Angeles California.

Two years later Nicholas was born, another son Alexander would follow shortly after that and by January 16, 1976 their family would be complete with the birth of their daughter Claire Elizabeth.

Robert was an Engineer and Jane was a Health care professional as well as a successful business woman. She made a six figure salary from her 9-5 job alone, and the horse ranch she ran with her daughter was starting to bring in money too.

Robert and Jane would have more than one argument over the money Jane and their daughter Claire spent on Charisma Ranch. He quit his job as an engineer to support Jane's endeavor of raising and training horses. Bob started a business making horse jumps, but by 2000 his business was in trouble. One of the last arguments Jane and Bob had was when Jane and Claire told him they found another horse that would be perfect for the ranch. Robert complained they didn't need any more horses. This infuriated Jane and she told him in no uncertain terms that it was her money and she would spend it how she wanted, she didn't need his permission.

On the afternoon of February 13, 2000 Jane got ready to go down to tend to the horses. Bob was dressing in his jogging clothes and told Jane he was going to go for a run. Bob had been a long distance runner for years. Jane had an injury that prevented her from participating. Jane asked her husband to stoke the fire before he left and she went to the barn.

Mrs. Dorotik returned to the house a couple hours later and Bob was nowhere to be found. She waited a while longer and began looking for him. There were others including neighbors and sons Nick and Alex. Becoming increasingly worried about her husband Jane called the police and told them that he had not come home after his run. A search was organized by the police and in the early morning hours of February 14, 2000 Police found Robert's battered, bloodied body by the side of the road about three miles from home. Police immediately suspected Jane.

Robert Dorotik had died from blunt force trauma and strangulation. He had several injuries to the face and the back of the head (an expert testified the wounds were consistent with a hammer). There were defensive wounds on his hands. He was still wearing his jogging clothes although according to the detectives his shoes were tied in an odd manner. The rope used to strangle him was still around his neck and had made a laceration on his throat.

They did not find blood at the scene that would have been consistent with it being the murder site. Robert had been killed somewhere else and moved here. They found the tire tracks and shoe prints. Jane could not be linked to any of the shoe prints, only the tire tracks. However, hers were not the only tire tracks there, the others were not linked to anyone.

The evidence from the beginning seemed to point at Jane Dorotik as the killer. At the scene where they found the body there were tire tracks that matched the three different treads on her truck. At the residence there was a massive amount of blood that had been cleaned at. Jane claims that the blood was from a nosebleed Robert had and cleaned up. Between the box springs and mattress there was a towel soaked with blood. In a bag in the master bedroom they found a syringe with a horse tranquilizer in it and Jane's fingerprint in Bob's blood was found on it. She was arrested before the blood analysis could even be returned.

Around the room investigators found impact blood spatter patterns as well as drip, transfer and cast off. In one of the closets in the house they found a steam carpet shampooer and a significant amount of cleaning supplies. Bob's blood was found on the cap, handle and nozzle of one of the bottles.

Blood stains consistent with Robert's were found in the bed of the truck Jane, Claire and the ranch hands used around the ranch. They found no blood spatter on his shoes or shirt, but did find some blood on his boxers. One of the two hands never showed up for work the day after Bob's death.

Jane was booked into San Diego County Jail and with the help of family made bail.

Jane's daughter Claire was incriminated in the murder, that she was actually the one that killed Robert, her own father. It was well known that father and daughter had a stormy relationship, and at times became volatile. It was never revealed why the two seemed to hate each other, but Claire even wrote a scathing letter to her father about a "betrayal of trust."

Jane's defense team Kerry Steigerwalt and Cole Casey now had to figure out how to defend their 55 year old client. What they decided on wasn't the most unusual way to do it and it and many other attorneys had done in numerous courtrooms around the country. They deliberately brought Claire up as a suspect. By showing that another person 'could' have committed the murder there is a chance that it will raise enough of a doubt in a jury's mind for them to bring back an acquittal instead of a guilty verdict. This is what the attorney's for Jane were doing, trying to raise a reasonable doubt. This strategy would ultimately tear the family apart. In a letter written three years after her conviction Jane would call her attorney 'ego driven' and the implicating of her daughter a 'seriously flawed defense strategy.'

Prosecutor Bonnie Howard-Regan was convinced that Jane killed her husband to keep from having to pay him spousal support. It seemed there was an impending divorce on the horizon for Bob and Jane. They had separated in 1997 but talked it out and decided to keep their money separate and got back together.

Their own sons commented that their parents' marriage wasn't the most loving and at times their fights became very heated. But is this a motive for murder? Perhaps not just the fights, maybe it was the fact that if the two divorced Jane would have to pay Robert up to 40% of her annual income. This would be upwards of 50,000 dollars a year. Jane was incensed when a divorce attorney had told her that. That is a huge motive for murder in the eyes of the law. There was also a $250,000 life insurance policy on both Bob and Jane. She was forthcoming with the detectives about this during the investigation. If she had to pay that much out in spousal support she wouldn't be able to keep the horse ranch, and it seemed that was all she cared about.

Jane's trial would begin in May of 2001 a little over a year after her husband was murdered. Jane had pled not guilty and was making passionate pleas to the public declaring her innocence. Though her daughter and sister also claimed that Jane was innocent of this heinous crime, Claire, Bonnie Long and a ranch hand all invoked their Fifth Amendment right against self-incrimination. Steigerwalt brought up the fact that Claire's alibi was never confirmed. Had the Sheriff's Department zeroed in on Jane in a hasty attempt to close the case?

On June 9, 2001 the case of Jane Dorotik v The State of California went to the jury for deliberation. After the third day both the defense and the prosecution were starting to worry. Maybe they hadn't presented their case as well as they'd thought. Maybe they didn't explain things in an easy to understand way. In the end however, it wasn't that the jury had a problem understanding what they saw and heard during the trial. They were just being diligent, making sure every juror understood what the evidence was and how it fit in the scheme of things. In fact, they had a unanimous decision on the first vote...guilty on the charge of first degree murder.

Judge Joan Weber said that there was "an overwhelming amount of circumstantial evidence" and when Jane's attorney filed for a new trial it was denied. New witnesses had come forward and Steigerwalt asked that the case be reopened to the jury could hear what they had to say. She denied his request. Weber also asked, "How could you have your husband's blood on your hands if you had nothing to do with his death?" The Judge Weber was referring to the syringe with Janes fingerprint on it. It was an integral piece of evidence in the case.

Without a new trial in San Diego County, the next step is Court Of Appeal Of California, Fourth Appellate District, Division One.

The Court of Appeals works differently than the Trial Court. It is not a place for a new trial or a retrial. They won't look at new evidence or hear from new witnesses. It is strictly for trying to overturn the lower court's decision. If this happens then the Trial Court would be made to do one of several different actions in the case. One would be a whole new trial, which in Jane's case is what her attorney would want to happen. Or perhaps the Appellate Court would order Trial Court to look at additional evidence and/or revisit the facts in the case.

Either of these would be a win for Jane and her defense team. However, before these could happen her attorney would have to show that there was an error in the trial procedure or in how Weber interpreted the law.

This all starts with a Notice to Appeal, and then a brief has to be filed. In many cases appeals are decided based solely on this brief. Other times there will oral arguments before anything is decided.

Janes appeal was filed on November 18, 2003. She is asserting that Judge Weber should have included in the instructions to the jury the lessor charge of voluntary manslaughter because the state didn't present evidence that there was premeditation and aforethought to constitute first degree murder. She was denied.

On June 12, 2009 Jane filed another appeal. There were three key facts in this appeal. In the first one she claims 'ineffective assistance of counsel'. Jane claimed that her defense team didn't represent her properly. They didn't do any investigation of their own.

Second, she believed that not letting the jury hear from the new witnesses and not doing DNA testing jeopardized her case. The rope used to strangle Robert was never test for DNA, claiming that epithelia's of the real killer would have been found.

Third, there were procedural mistakes because of the delayed discovery and her actual innocence.

The defense was not allowed to present evidence that the State's expert witness had many mistakes in other cases by using 'faulty methodology'. The jury was not allowed to hear from an eyewitness.

The Appellate Court denied her, again.

The San Diego Union-Tribune reported on November 22, 2015 that a Judge has determined Jane be allowed to have the DNA in her case tested. The rope used to strangle Bob, the fingernail scrapings, and a piece of hair found around the victim's finger all be tested.

Jane still proclaims her innocence and said the ranch hand that didn't show up for work the day after the murder should be considered. He drives a black pick-up, and his tire tracks were also found at the scene. She also reiterated that the man owed the Dorotik's money.

Jane filed her first appeal on November 18, 2003. The Appellate court upheld the lower court's decision. Then Jane, known also as the petitioner filed Habeas petition on April 4, 2006 in the State Superior Court. Next was a Habeas Petition in the Appellate Court on January 3, 2006. And again Jane filed with the State Supreme Court on November 20, 2006. All appeals and motions to this point had been denied or affirmed the lower court's decision.

On June 1, 2007 Jane would file a Petition for Writ of Habeas Corpus, a Motion to appoint counsel, a Motion for Leave to Proceed in Forma Pauperis and a request for DNA testing. This too was denied or dismissed.

In July of 2007 Jane managed to get the money for filing fees and Magistrate Judge Porter ordered the case be reopened on July 9, 2007.

In the appeal for ineffectual assistance of counsel the superior court "denied the claims on the merits in a written order but only addressed the first two claims. On appeal the Appellate Court did the same thing.

Jane contends that council should have done independent testing of the forensic evidence that the prosecution would be presenting at trial and that there was other available evidence that he could have taken advantage of but didn't. Jane contends that had he done so the findings would have weakened the prosecution's case.

Another point the petitioner brought up is that her counsel didn't call her as a witness in her own defense.

Petitioner wanted a medical professional called as an expert witness to testify as to the medical impossibility that she could have perpetrated the murder due to an injury from an accident years earlier. That she would not have had the strength to do what the prosecution says she did.

Counsel for the defense did not object when a detective testified that he thought she was the killer. He could have also asked for a mistrial also.

He didn't insist on DNA testing prior to the start of the trial, armed with the results of the tests, petitioner is sure that it would have pointed to the real killer or killers.

Petitioner believes that her counsel should have brought up different scenarios that could have explained away the circumstantial evidence brought up at trial.

That he could have provided innocent theories for the incriminating evidence.

He didn't show that police didn't follow any leads, including eyewitnesses that came forward in the early stages of the investigation; they made up their mind that she was guilty. Therefore they didn't look for the real killer/killers.

Jane contends that her counsel could have done their own investigation and found the witnesses that were not heard at trial. Instead he made the leap to blaming Claire Dorotik as a defense.

And finally, follow through on the promises counsel made to the jury about what the evidence would show, and not make a comment to the affect that Jane was guilty.

If none of these ten points were true but the last one, would that fact that her own defense counsel made a comment that directly or indirectly told the jury he thought she was guilty should have been grounds for a mistrial and perhaps proceedings started to disbar her attorney.

The points brought up in Jane's eyes caused her to be wrongly convicted for the murder of her husband.

The forensic evidence in many parts does not support the prosecution's theory. Think about the "blood" found on the wall that supposedly dripped down from the master bedroom upstairs. The man who sold /rented the property to the Dorotik's knew of a water leak. Rain water would get in the track of the sliding door and seep down the wall of the stairs leading to the bedroom. There was Bob's DNA there, but was it from blood? Walking shirtless up the stairs and rubbing his sweaty arm on the wall could leave his DNA, it was not said that it was blood.

Post-conviction reports showed that there was way less blood present than would have been if the State's expert witness, Merrit, were correct. McDonell who did the post-conviction report says the fatal blow probably occurred outside the bedroom. But at the same time doesn't accept the idea that Bob was killed where he was found or that he was killed somewhere else, body dumped where it was found and the blood evidence planted.

McDonell also said that the blood on the mattress could have easily been caused by a bloody nose. That being said it still doesn't explain the different blood stain patterns found throughout the room. Those where found on the pillow, nightstand, walls, bedspread and the window. Those he said cannot be explained away by a nosebleed.

The post-conviction report says that Merrit's testimony was wrong inasmuch as there was not enough blood soaked in to support his idea that Bob remained on the mattress for a long time after the attack.

McDonell concurs with petitioner that the blood around the pot-belly stove could very well have been from the nosebleed. Petitioner wants further testing to find out if it even had anything to do with the murder at all.

The bloody thumb print on the syringe was due to Bob helping Jane with a vet procedure. There was a horse tranquilizer inside the syringe and Jane's thumbprint in Bob's blood on it. This was admitted into evidence? Why, it's said to be a 'key piece' of evidence in the prosecution's case. Petitioner's counsel didn't object? Per Bob's toxicology report there was no drugs in his system. How did they tie it into the murder?

The truck, tire tracks and shoe prints. There was much to do about the tire tracks at the scene where Bob's body was found. There were actually two sets, one belonging to the family truck, the one that everyone including the farm hands had access to. But there was another set, never identified. The shoe prints found also at the scene couldn't be attributed to Jane either. Both sets were too big. The tracks that showed Jane's truck had backed up at the spot where the body was found can easily be explained as well. Bob used the truck to measure jogging routes. If he were to come to the exact length he wanted, he would have just turned around at that spot, hence the backup tracks.

A cursory search of the house was done the evening that Jane reported Bob missing. Police and Police dogs were all in the house including the master bedroom. They didn't find any blood.

Jane was in an accident in 1983 and had a severe injury to a hip which had to be put back together with metal and screws. The prosecution says that Jane would have bludgeoned her husband, then carried him down the stairs from the bedroom, through the house, across a 60' porch and lifted him into the back of a full sized Ford

F250. Defense counsel should have brought up the fact that his client couldn't have done any of that. The Appellate court says that her sons saw her pulling irrigation pipes around the ranch that weighed about 75 lbs. pulling on 75lbs of something is different than lifting 147 lbs of dead weight.

Detective Richard Empson when questioned about the rope used to strangle Robert Dorotik and why it wasn't tested for DNA said the "criminologists in his office discouraged testing it because too many people had handled it." When pressed about the possibility of DNA on it that could have belonged to Claire or the ranch hand Leonel Morales or someone else and lead to the real killer, what then? Empson continued, "I believe I know who killed Bob Dorotik, that's why I arrested Jane Dorotik." Personal opinions are not supposed to be brought in to testimony, especially from an officer of the court. Did Jane's counsel object to this? Did it prejudice the jury against the petitioner? It could be said that it inflamed the jury. Most jurors will believe a law enforcement officer over anyone else. Even if the comment was objected to and stricken from the record the juror's still heard it and no matter if they are told to disregard it, it will still be in their mind.

There are so many points that Jane brought up on each one of her appeals. And each and every one of them were dismissed by the Courts. Many of Jane's friends and family still believe that Jane is innocent and should at least get a new trial so all of the evidence can be heard and that maybe she can even testify in her own defense. Although her trial court attorney believed that doing so was not a good idea. Clearly he didn't believe his client was innocent of the crime.

In the findings of the Appellate Court they say that the petitioner didn't show how not having the jury hear that Merrit's methodology was flawed and that he had been wrong on other cases would not have changed the jury's verdict.

They stated that even though the petitioner believes that the prosecution purposefully did not test for DNA she cannot prove how it would have changed anything. Also added the testing would not have brought forth any exculpatory or impeaching evidence. Knowing that DNA has set wrongfully convicted people free by proving their innocence this statement seems wrong in its entirety. Jane would be in a Catch 22 scenario, she can't prove that by not testing there was an error in law and without being able to prove it would help her case they wouldn't allow the testing.

Jane says she's been through a living hell since being sent to Chowchilla's prison facility in central California. But she hasn't been wasting her time. Along with filing the above mentioned appeals she is fighting for her fellow prisoners who are over the age of 55.

Jane is appalled at how many women are incarcerated and how the number keeps growing every year. She was once a mental health professional and says that a large number of women in prison should be in a Mental Health facility.

According to Jane "Medical care is liken to a third world country." And "there are women dying in prison alone and unnoticed by prison staff.

What she is trying to get done is this, have more compassionate releases, the parole board has the authority to do this but won't. So a program is working its way through legislation in the state of California. "If The Risk Is Low, Let Them Go".

Jane isn't advocating opening the flood gates and letting these women head off to parts unknown. There are a certain set of criteria in place to make sure the risk is actually low.

First of all, they have to have served at least 50% of their sentence or seven years.

They can't have had any disciplinary actions in the past five years. In other words they have to be a model prisoner.

They cannot have any other felony convictions of their record and they must have a concrete, safe place to stay in the community

These are safeguards to keep reoffenders inside the prison walls. Jane is very passionate about this program. She has watched many of what she calls "Golden Girls" languishing with terminal illnesses for years, alone, not able to be with family because Chowchilla houses inmates from all over the state.

Many of the families just don't have the money or time to be able to travel to see their loved ones. And even the children have to be patted down before they can go in to see a relative, to possibly say a last goodbye.

Jane's alternative custody program has to clear through law makers and with the help of different advocates it's headed in the right direction thanks to Carol Lui a senator from California.

This is being heralded as a great program to help with overcrowding of the prisons in California, and if this comes about in a timely manner it could help Jane as well. She is now 68 years old.

BRITTNEY JANE DWYER

At nineteen years of age, Brittney Jane Dwyer developed an obsession with horror movies and television shows. Brittney has always a taste for violence and the darker side of life, but her family never noticed a lack of empathy. She grew up with a stable household and loving family. "She was a strong-willed, adventures, tom-boy growing up," says her mother Tonya Dwyer. During her high school years, she developed a close bond with a school friend named Shelby Lee Holmes, but she spent the majority of her time alone. Brittney isolated herself as a teenager and did not fit in with a popular crowd. Brittney seemed to be a relatively normal girl up until she became addicted to drugs and murdered her eighty-one-year-old grandfather in cold blood.

Brittney had moved out of her parent's household and she was living with her (what she called) girlfriend Bernadette Burns and their two roommates. The girls were short on money and they did whatever they could to round up a couple of bucks. Knowing that Brittney's family had money accessible to her, robbery became their newest obsession. Brittney and Bernadette drove across Australia in the search for Brittney's grandfather's life savings. The girls were living in Queensland Australia when they decided to move forward with robbery. They were motivated to steal money in order to support their erratic lifestyle and drug habit. Brittney's grandfather, Robert Whitwell, was living in Adelaide Australia at the time of his murder. This was quite a way away from Queensland. In the past months, Brittney overheard her grandfather and mother speaking about her grandfather's savings. Robert confessed to keeping his life savings on his premise, due to his distrust in the banking system. Although Brittney's mother attempted to convince Robert to put his money in a secure savings account he denied. With this knowledge, Brittney and Bernadette set off on their mission.

Robert Whitwell was a friendly gentleman who had been through many hurdles in his lifetime. Whitwell lived through the Great Depression and he saw the effects on banks and their sneaky tactics. After the Great Depression, many people found it difficult to regain their trust in the banking system, this included Robert Whitwell. During the Great Depression, the banks were overleveraged, and many people had their money lent out to other people in loans. This led to more and more people withdrawing their money and hiding it in their homes. Hiding their money gave them a sense of security, it made them feel as if they held control over their money. The older generations were very creative in where they hid their money. The most common places that the elderly would hide their money were, in the attic, indoors, behind vents, in pianos, in the shed, stuffed in cabinets, and stuffed in the backyard. Robert Whitwell chose to hide his money in his backyard shed. This was his way of knowing that his money was safe, and he had control of his savings. Robert did not have to worry about the bank. His money was hidden in plain sight and well enough that those close to him were unable to find it. Brittney knew that his money was somewhere on the property, but she did not overhear exactly where the money was.

All Brittney knew about her Grandfather's money was that he had around 110,000 dollars and it was hidden on his property. Brittney was willing to do whatever it took to take this money, even if this meant brutally murdering her own grandfather. On August 5, 2016, Brittney and Bernadette arrived at Robert Whitwell's home at approximately 11:00 am. Brittney and Bernadette had been texting about this very moment for weeks as they planned their excursion. The girls had sent over 1,900 texts to one another over the course of a two-year period. When they arrived at Robert Whitwell's house the girls talked briefly before Brittney went inside. Bernadette waited in the car while Brittney went inside to see her grandad equipped with rubber gloves and a knife. According to Brittney, Bernadette was doing her makeup while Brittney was inside.

Robert Whitwell was excited to see his granddaughter at his doorstep that morning. He was quick to invite her in for breakfast. Most grandparents live for the moment's they get to spend with their grandchildren, and Robert was one of those grandfathers. Robert treasured his family and he was described as a man who welcomed anyone, he was a true gentleman. Robert opened his door believing that he was going to enjoy time with his granddaughter. A time where he could tell her story of his past and reminisce over old photographs. What Robert Whitwell did not realize was that his granddaughter had a very different motive behind her visit. When Robert opened the door, he led his granddaughter into the house where they enjoyed breakfast. They later moved to the living room where they looked at a photo album filled with pictures of Brittney and her brother as young children. During this time together Brittney began to question her ability to follow through with her plan. She texted Bernadette saying she could not go through with "it". She was questioning the idea of murder and robbery when she saw how gentle and genuine her grandfather was. Bernadette responded by texting her back "We had come all this way". This one, very simple text convinced Brittney to finish what she was there to do.

As Brittney's visit with her grandfather was coming to an end, he walked her towards the front door. At the front door, Brittney pulled out her knife that was waiting in her pocket. She took the knife and without hesitation, stabbed her grandfather. Initially, she stabbed him in the chest and then she stabbed him a second time in the neck. Ruthlessly, she followed her grandfather back to the kitchen where he fell to the floor. He was reaching for a band-aid and Brittney helped him find one and apply it to his wound. Brittney knew that her grandfather was going to die but she still helped him apply a bandage to his bleeding wound. The last thing her grandfather did was ask

Brittney, "Why?". Rather than answering her grandfather, she left him to bleed out on the floor while she took out her rubber gloves and began to wash the dishes. She continued with the dishes silently, until she was reassured that her grandfather was in fact dead. After she confirmed that he was gone she texted Bernadette who was waiting outside. She sent a message that was made up of two words "It's done". This is when the search for the money began. Brittney and Bernadette began searching the house and all of its nooks and crannies. After a thorough search, they only found 1,000 dollars in cash. When they felt that they had exhausted all of the search options they left with the money, a few coins, and two digital cameras.

An hour after leaving Robert Whitwell's house Bernadette made a post on Facebook about the situation. Her post read, "The story of my life, I knew better but I did it anyway". When the girls returned from their trip their roommates questioned where they had been. They had been living with Jodie Greaves and Jamie Dennis up until the murder of Robert Whitwell. Bernadette told their roommates that they returned to the apartment after her Uncle had died in a home invasion in Perth. Bernadette's story was not that convincing as she later made a secret confession to Jodie about what really happened on their trip. "I recall Jamie saying to her that was a bit random, but she approached me and said, 'Can I tell you something, but you can't tell anyone but Jamie?' She went on to tell me that her and Brittney's trip to Adelaide was for the purpose of robbing her (Brittney's) grandad. Bernadette said that before they set off on that trip, Brittney made a joke to her that she was going to kill her grandad, but Bernadette told me she did not think she was serious at first" Says Jodie in her police statement. Bernadette continued to tell her roommates about the fatality that happened when visiting Brittney's grandfather. "Bernadette told me she had a go at Brittney as she had spent all their money on fuel to get them to Adelaide and then couldn't go through with anything. She went on to tell me that she sat in the car discussing things with Brittney for about twenty minutes and then Brittney changed her mind and went into her granddad's house. Bernadette said that Brittney had her breakfast with her granddad and then she killed him. I asked if she was joking and she said "no", and she burst into tears and started to cry uncontrollably" Jodie exclaimed.

Bernadette pleaded guilty to murder in front of the Supreme Court Justice Trish Kelly. Rather than letting the case go to a trial she confessed and was sentenced. She pled guilty for committing an intentional act of violence while undertaking the robbery, which resulted in the death of Robert Whitwell. This type of offense is similar to felony murder and it carries the same sentence of life in prison. The Supreme Court Justice stated, "In the case against Burns, Ms. Telfer said her involvement was at the lower end of the scale". Bernadette Burn's lawyer Anthony Allen informed the court that after the sentencing his client would be deported, due to the fact that Bernadette was not an Australian citizen. Bernadette asked her lawyer to speak on her behalf when the court was in session. "She feels great shame and sorrow for what she did. Through me, she says that she is sorry" says Anthony.

Three days after the girls finished their robbery and murder Robert Whitwell's driveway began to fill up with newspapers. This was unusual for Mr. Whitwell as he was very meticulous about his house and his garden. His neighbors became concerned about his well-being and they entered the house to find him on the floor, dead. The police were called immediately, and the investigation was started. Forensic officers conducted a post mortem report to understand exactly what went into Robert Whitwell's death. According to the Detective Chief Inspector Shane Addison "It appeared that Mr. Whitwell's death was from not from natural causes but there were several factors we cannot yet explain". At the initial time of the investigation, the police were unable or unwilling to share what these factors were. The police put out a statement to the media stating that Mr. Whitwell's death was being investigated as unexplained and they were looking for help answering questions related to his death. In the police statement police also said "Mr. Whitwell was last seen by neighbors on Thursday, August 4, 2016, and he was in contact with family the following morning. We are keen to talk to anyone who knows him, is a friend or has seen him recently as investigators are keen to establish his recent movements. Police will also conduct further investigation into this unexplained death to determine the circumstances behind it." Police did not want to disclose the nature of Robert Whitwell's death to the media during the initial investigation.

Robert Whitwell's death was not declared a major crime at the time of his finding, but his death was described as being "Shocking". The fact that the door was left unlocked and accessible for neighbors to walk inside was bringing up many different questions. One of these questions was, did Mr. Whitwell know the person who last saw him alive? Forensic testing eventually led the police all the way to Queensland City Australia, where they arrested Brittney Jane Dwyer and Bernadette Burns. The fact that both women were visiting South Australia on the day of Robert Whitwell's death was very unusual. Both women were set to appear at the Brisbane Magistrates Court just days after they were arrested. Police had asked for an extradition request due to the nature of the crime, which was granted. When the women appeared in court, they were both formally charged with the murder of Robert Whitwell.

During Brittney Jane Dwyer's second court appearance she confessed to the murder of her grandfather. Both Brittney and Bernadette plead guilty to murder at their presentencing hearing. In Brittney's initial confession she claimed that the hit television show American Horror Story motivated her to complete her grandfather's slaying. According to Brittney's lawyer Craig Caldicott, the television show explores humankind's capacity for evil and they put a heavy focus on crime and the act of murder. The show is an anthology that is based on different crimes that are being committed by different characters in different situations. Every season of American Horror Story depicts a completely different story and the seasons include, a house with a murderous past, an insane asylum, a witch's coven, freak show/circus, a hotel, a farmhouse, a cult, and the apocalypse. It was also during this time that Brittney was set up to speak to a psychiatrist as she was previously diagnosed with Borderline personality disorder. In her confession, she also stated that she was using an excessive amount of drugs. According to her both her lawyer and psychiatrist she was exaggerating. According to Brittney, she was smoking an ounce of marijuana a day. This is something that even the most dedicated cannabis users would not smoke. On average one person can smoke about one ounce of marijuana a week. Brittney also claimed that when she smoked, she would drink a complete bottle of vodka and cap it off with both cocaine and ecstasy.

Brittney had hoped that her Borderline Personality Disorder and excessive drug usage would help her case in court, but much of what she said was an exaggeration. She tried to say that her mental disorder and drug usually played a role in her crime. She also made several claims about her grandfather sexually abusing her. According to psychiatrists, this was most likely false. Brittney was giving different information to the authorities and her psychiatrists. It was difficult to find the entire truth within her statements. Each version of her confessions was thoroughly investigated and the alleged claims that her grandfather had sexually abused her as a child were proven to be false. Brittney's lawyer attempted to ask for leniency from the judge due to Brittney's young age and her "troubled youth". "Ms. Dwyer had a very troubled upbringing on the outside, it appeared that she was in a loving family relationship but there were aspects of self-harm that lead her into a life of drug taking," said Caldicott. He then asked the judge for leniency in sentencing when determining her non-parole period due to her age. "She was nineteen years old at the time... we have a very, very young woman" he said.

The prosecutor in the Dwyer case dismissed many of Brittney's stories stating that her alleged sexual abuse was an unpleasant emotion, but it was unfounded. Prosecutor Emily Telfer described the murder as being "heinous" and it should be treated as a very serious offense. According to Telfer, the fact that Brittney gave different versions of events to multiple different people advances her position at the time. "It is difficult to know what to accept from what she says because of the different version of events. There has never been an expression of real remorse" says Telfer. The judge took all of this into consideration during their sentencing and he questioned Brittney's upbringing and whether or not her lawyer's statement of a "difficult" upbringing was true or not. According to Justice Nicholson, he thought that she had a relatively normal upbringing, and this was not a factor in her crime. According to the justice, there were no extreme factors other than Brittney's extreme youth. There was nothing that gave the judge any reason to be lenient with Brittney's sentencing. This is when the judge began to question Brittney's ability to empathize with others, especially with her crime being sociopathic in nature. When Brittney was faced with her friends and family as they made their victim statements, she did not have much to say or emotion to show.

During the trial, many of Brittney's family were called upon to make statements. Her own mother found it difficult to be in front of her daughter, as she wondered where she went wrong as a parent. Her mother wondered what she didn't see as Brittney was growing up or what signs she missed. Her mother remembers her as a normal child the only thing that was out of the ordinary was her visits to the cemetery, but there was nothing that pointed to her future killing. Days after her Brittney murdered her grandfather she sat with the family, crying. Her mom asked her "what didn't I see". Brittney's brother had similar feelings as his mother, and he wondered what he could have to prevent this horrific crime. "I think about what I could have done to stop it. The prosecutors described the killing as almost sociopathic in style."

He says. This was a difficult event for all of the members of Brittney's family as they did not lose one person, they lost two. Brittney's father was devastated and did not have much to say in his statement. He asked the judge to give Brittney the appropriate punishment for her crime. Gary Dwyer stated that he would always remember his father in law as being a gentleman and a man with a real love for his family. Many of Robert Whitwell's friends and family described him as being "meticulous" a loving man. Robert spent time in his garden making sure it was perfect and he would take baskets of vegetables to his neighbors as often as he could.

It was Robert's brothers and daughter who took his murder the hardest. Geoffrey Dwyer broke down as he entered the courtroom saying, "you couldn't ask for a better brother". Geoffrey's official statement read, "Bob and I were very close. We always came together for Christmas and Bob's birthday was special because it was on the same day as my wife's birthday. I would speak on the phone with Bob frequently. But I will never hear the phone ring with my brother on the other end. (Speaking to Brittney) We welcomed you into our home, embraced you and comforted you, all while you wept with your fake tears and made comments like 'my poor papa'. I now know that I had been embracing and comforting my brother's killer. You are a master of deception; I will give you that. I will never forgive you. You are a cruel, deceitful person with no regard for human life – I believe you are dangerous and evil and deserve the highest penalty" Geoffrey read his statement with tears in his eyes and sadness around him, his statement was both powerful and impactful.

Geoffrey's statement was not the only statement that was directed at Brittny. Robert's daughter, Tonya Dwyer made an extremely impactful and statement. "Since the crime has taken place I have been on a rollercoaster of emotions, shock, grief, anger, and sadness. I feel like I am drowning in life. I can't concentrate through the day and I can't sleep at night. The images of what my father went through in his last minutes of life consume me with sadness. I had been a happy wife, mother, and daughter until everything changed. Now I feel like I'm drowning in life. How is it fair that you can still spend a loving moment with your father, and I had to bury mine? No words can describe the pain I feel knowing you helped to put this in place." read Tonya. As the victims read each statement Brittney stood there with no emotional response. Tonya was another family member who asked the judge for "appropriate" justice.

After the judge listened to all statements pertaining to the case, he had a lot to say about the crime. Justice Nicholson had to consider whether Dwyer was a dangerous person to society. "She leaves school and goes crazy in terms of her lifestyle. There are no mitigating factors except for her extreme youth. I have to consider whether Dwyer is a very dangerous person, who at eighteen has gone from zero to premeditated murder. This was not a crime of passion, there's no alcohol or drugs involved, this is just a straight out, I'm going to do it. When someone is of that nature it's hard to measure contrition. It may be that she is not capable of it which is a worrying factor" Nicholson said. Through this time Brittney had shown no remorse to her friends or her family, she did not acknowledge just how much she had hurt them. The only sense of remorse that Brittney tried to show was in one statement "I am sorry, and I would take it back if I could" says Brittney. Even this statement was not one hundred percent authentic as she said this via her lawyer. Her lawyer Caldicott claimed that Brittney was distraught over the murder and she knows that he actions have caused her to lose her grandfather, family, and girlfriend (although, Bernadette refused to acknowledge that they were a couple).

The question remains, is Brittney Jane Dwyer a sociopath as described by the court and her family. A sociopath is a person who lacks any emotion or empathy towards anyone else, they emotionally destroy anyone who is close to them. The way that they destroy a person is consistent with their approach to other people. They kill a person just like someone would kill a character in a video game. Many sociopaths suffer from a lack of social obligations, moral anchors, and the ability to create and maintain a relationship. A true sociopath may appear to be charming; this is a personality disorder that affects the facets of each person's inner and outer worlds. It is unclear whether or not Brittney Jane Dwyer is a sociopath, but the court has proven that she has sociopathic tendencies and she is a danger to society due to how she murdered her grandfather. Even though the murder was pre-meditated it was acted out with a lack of regard for anyone in her family. She was able to carry out a violent stabbing and watch her grandfather die while casually doing the dishes. These are all variables that the court took into account when deciding on Brittney's sentence.

Brittney Jane Dwyer was eventually sentenced to life in prison. Supreme Court Justice Kevin Nicholson sentenced Britney to prison with a non-parole period of 20.5 years for the murder of her grandfather Robert Whitwell. He also added an additional six months to her sentence for home invasion. At the time of sentencing, Brittney was 20 years old and she will not be eligible for parole for 21 years, making her 41 years old when she becomes eligible for parole. Her co-conspirator was also sentenced to life in prison, but the judge found her as not having an intent to murder. Bernadette Burns will not be eligible for parole for 13.5 years, 7.5 years earlier then Brittney. At the end of the sentencing Robert's brother Geoffrey left the court, the media, and his family with a final statement, "I hope that the family will come together to support one another." He said. "We just have to know and be glad it's all over and we can get closure. Let the healing begin. It's a test upon everybody in the family. You've just got to pick yourself up and do the best you can and get on with life. I hope that is what all the members of the family do." Brittney's family has struggled to come to turn with Brittney's ruthless killing and the betrayal of her own family members.

HUSBAND KILLER : THE TRUE STORY OF KELLY GISSENDANER

40

JENNIFER KENDALL

Kelly Gissendaner, born Kelly Brookshire, became the sixth and last woman executed in Georgia for her role in the murder of her husband, Douglas Gissendaner, by her lover, Greg Owen. The murder was gruesome, Kelly demonstrated a lack of credibility with lies, and the murder was clearly premeditated- three things that helped a jury convict her of her role in the murder. What hurt her the most, though, was that her former lover turned on her and testified against her. Kelly seemingly changed her life in prison, mentoring and preaching to other women. Her legal team appealed the decision due to a lack of proof, her redemption, and her relationship with her children. The mother of three children cried and sang "Amazing Grace" as she received the lethal injection and one hundred people protested her death outside.

Early Life

In 1968, Kelly Brookshire was born to Maxine and Marry Brookshire in Georgia. She has a brother that was born one year after Kelly. Kelly and her brother were not born into wealth or emotional stability. Her family consisted of simple cotton farmers. Her parents drank, did drugs, and fought. Due to the troubled relationship, they did not stay together. Kelly's father left the family and created a new one with no intention of including Kelly into his new family dynamic. This obviously left Kelly feeling unwanted and abandoned. Kelly's mother did remarry a man named Billy Wade eight days after the divorce with Kelly's father was final, but Billy only added more trauma to Kelly's already broken home. Many people came forward with knowledge of sexual abuse to Kelly by her stepfather and other men. On top of the sexual abuse, Billy Wade was physically and emotionally abusive to Kelly, her brother, and her mother. Luckily, her mother also divorced Billy Wade and moved the family.

Kelly stood at six feet tall, and she was rather homely looking. Many people made fun of her for her looks and being "trailer trash". She would prefer to work rather than socialize, mostly due to her household's financial situation and her mother's strict rules. Her first job was at McDonald's. She mostly kept to herself, but the outcast made one friend in a woman named Mitzi.

First child and marriage

Kelly got pregnant with her first child before she finished high school. She claimed that the child was conceived through date rape, and the father was not actively involved in the child's life. She refused to name the father to even her best friends. She also tried to hide the pregnancy for as long as she could, but the reality became apparent around her sixth month. Before she gave birth, her father reached out to her and suggested that she name the child with his last name. Her first child, Brandon Brookshire, was born in June of 1986. Kelly married her first husband, Jeff Banks, at the young age of nineteen, but the marriage only lasted for six months before it dissolved. Reports indicate that the marriage quickly ended when Kelly's father threatened Jeff with a gun for not passing him bread at the dinner table. After the marriage ended, Kelly and her baby moved into her mother's trailer. This was a rough time for Kelly, but she was saved when she met Douglas Gissendaner.

Marriage to Douglas Gissendaner

On September 2, 1989, Kelly became Mrs. Douglas Gissendaner... for the first time. Kelly was four months pregnant on her wedding day, which could have encouraged the nuptials. The marriage was tumultuous from the beginning. They had financial difficulty after they both lost their jobs and were forced to live with Doug's parents for some time. However, Doug provided a good life for Kelly and her child when he decided to enlist in the United States Army. Despite a steady paycheck, Kelly used the money irresponsibly and needed Doug's family to help her with car payments. Doug's parents already didn't love Kelly, and this added to their distrust. When Doug moved to Germany because of his job in the army, it only added to the tension. The move happened only one month after Kelly had given birth to their first child together and her second child, Kayla. When Kelly and Doug were together, they were noticeably miserable. The relationship did not work at all, and they fought constantly. People also spoke up about Kelly's partying and sleeping around with other men while Doug wasn't around. This caused even more strain on the family, and the couple divorced in 1993. This time, Kelly joined the army with no other way to support herself and her children, but she discovered that she was not made for the army. During this time, Kelly became pregnant with another man and gave birth to her final child Jonathan who everyone called Cody. This father would die of cancer shortly after his birth. After returning from the army, Kelly and Doug reconciled. Despite having a child with another man, they didn't want to separate their family. They remarried in May of 1995 and, despite a separation during this time, bought a house together in Auburn, Georgia in December of 1996. A few months later, Doug was murdered.

Greg Owen

While divorced from Doug, Kelly started working for the International Readers League of Atlanta. At this time, she started socializing with her boss, Belinda Owens. When she met Belinda's brother Greg Owen, they had an instant chemistry. The relationship started strong, but it soon started to worry Belinda. Belinda noticed an alarming amount of fighting, and she didn't appreciate the bossy tone that Kelly used when she spoke to her brother. Kelly and Greg broke up, and Kelly went back to Doug and remarried. Kelly and Greg rekindled their romance during a brief separation between Kelly and Douglas, but Kelly ultimately stayed married to Douglas. Many suspect her devotion to her relationship with Doug involved stability for her and her children rather than love. This was only amplified by the fact that many reports indicated that she continued to maintain a relationship with Owen throughout her marriage to Douglas.

Murder and Investigation

In February 7, 1997, Douglas Gissendaner was murdered by in a secluded part of rural Gwinnett County. Douglas came home from a friend's house shocked to find Gregory Owen in his home. Gregory then exhibited a knife and forced Douglas to drive to a remote area. When they stopped, Owen forced Douglas out of the car and made him walk 300 feet into the woods before beating him in the skull with a nightstick and repeatedly stabbing him in the neck and back. When Kelly arrived, she helped set the car on fire to eliminate any evidence.

The night of the murder, Kelly had gone out for dinner and drinks with friends. Despite dancing and having a good time, she went home right around midnight. Friends with her that night reported that she told them that she went home because she had a feeling that there was something wrong. Kelly frantically searched for Doug when he didn't come home the next day. She made several calls, but she reportedly could not locate him. She even called his parents to ask if they had seen him. That same day a missing person's report was created by the local police department, and they started their search immediately.

Investigators had trouble with Kelly's story from the start. When she spoke with them, she described her marriage as happy and noneventful, but other people provided reports of fighting and numerous problems including Kelly's infidelity. One name that came up over and over again in interviews with friends and family was Greg Owen.

Greg Owen seemed to have a reasonable alibi. A roommate stated that he was home all night and got picked up by a friend for work the following morning at 9:00 a.m. With his roommate's alibi, police put Greg's interrogation on hold and continued their investigation.

Investigators finally got a big clue when they found Doug's car. It was left on a rural road in Gwinnett County. The most interesting thing about finding the car was that it appeared to be burned from the inside. At this time, there was no sign of Doug. While the situation didn't look good for Doug, family and friends knew that police were getting closer to the truth.

The day that the car was found, friends and family gathered to the home of Doug Sr. and Sue Gissendaner to support them during this difficult time. Kelly made an appearance, but she didn't stay long. She decided instead to take her children to the circus. While some people can understand how the environment can be traumatic to the children and maybe Kelly wanted to protect them, people found her decision evasive and questionable. Also, shouldn't the children be allowed to mourn with their grandparents? To increase suspicion even more, Kelly went back to work only four days into the search for her missing husband. Her behavior confused people around her. Sure, she had bills to pay, but four days was very soon to go back to work. Many people thought that she was hiding something. Many more people reported a weird attitude for a woman who had a missing husband.

After an already excruciating twelve days for Doug's friends and family, Doug's body was finally found in a horrific condition a mile from where they had found his car. His body appeared to be a bag of trash at first. He was on his knees, bent over, with his face in the dirt. Twelve days of decomposition, the elements, and animal attacks made him virtually unrecognizable. Medical professionals used dental records to confirm that the body was indeed Doug Gissendaner. He had been stabbed four times in the head, neck, and back.

While there was a long list of potential suspects, investigators kept Kelly close. When they talked to her again to go over her initial statements, the pressure must have gotten to her. She finally admitted that she had spoken to Greg on occasion when he called her. She made it clear to police that she did not pursue any relationship with Greg, and he pursued her. She also admitted that she reconciled with Owen during a separation, and she told investigators that he said that he would kill Doug when he found that she was getting back together with him. At this time, she pointed the finger at Greg and police questioned him heavily. Their relationship was officially over.

With the investigation focused on Greg, Greg's roommate changed his story completely. He was afraid that his leis could get him in trouble, and he told the police a new story. In fact, he confessed to investigators that Greg had been gone the night before until 8 am the next morning. With Greg's alibi gone, investigators knew they were getting even closer to the truth.

Kelly's story was raveling apart as well when investigators pulled up phone records that showed 47 calls between the two. They also saw that Kelly initiated the calls 18 times, which goes against what she told them while interrogated that she only spoke to him because he constantly called her. Furthermore, the correspondence ended immediately after the murder. Why would they stop talking so suddenly for no reason? Her inconsistencies made her look bad to the investigators who were suspicious of her story from the beginning.

After more interrogation, Greg confessed to the murder after he was told that cooperation could prevent him from getting the death penalty. He proceeds to implicate Kelly to save himself. He explains how he and Kelly had an intimate relationship, and she told Greg that she wanted him to kill Doug after they settled into their new house. She even came up with alibis at this time. He goes on to describe the murder in detail. He stated that Kelly picked him up and allowed her into his house. She even gave him the nightstick and the knife that he would use to attack her husband. She advised him to make it look like a home invasion and robbery. Greg waited until Doug got home at around 11 pm, and then he forced him to drive out to the boondocks by knifepoint. They eventually stopped, and Greg forced Doug out of the car and told him to walk. He committed the horrible murder by hitting him in the head with the nightstick and then stabbing him repeatedly, leaving him to bleed. Once completed, Kelly arrived with kerosene to get rid of the evidence. After the murder, Kelly told Greg that they shouldn't speak anymore until things die down. This is the confession that Greg gave police. With this confession, Greg only received a sentence of twenty five years to life instead of the death penalty.

As soon as the police had Greg's confession, they went to also arrest Kelly. They barged into her home on February 25th and completed the arrest. Kelly changed her story once again after her arrest. She confessed that she saw Greg Owen the night of the murder. This time she said that he called her, and she went to pick him up. When he picked her up, he told her about the murder. He then proceeded to threated to murder her and her children as well if she did not help him. Even though the police didn't believe her, Kelly maintained her innocence. Greg was only lying to save himself! She even turned down the plea deal offered to her and decided to go to trial. It was the same plea deal that the prosecution gave Greg- a guilty plea would give her twenty five to life, but she would not get the death penalty. Even her lawyer suggested that she take the plea deal, but Kelly decided to go to trial.

Trial

The first day of Kelly's trial was on November 2, 1998. The jury consisted of two men and ten women. Reporters were prevalent throughout the proceedings.

Prosecutors started by painting a picture of a troubled marriage between Kelly and Doug and her affair with Greg Owen. They then claimed that Gissendaner killed her husband to receive the house he bought for the family and two $10,000 life insurance policies. The reward was surprisingly small but substantial enough to be considered a motive alongside her affair. Prosecution also pointed out inconsistencies in her police reports of the night and the fact that Kelly specifically waited until Doug had bought the house for her and her children. She even had the foresight to plan alibis. This indicated that the murder was premeditated.

The prosecution brought many people into court to testify against Kelly. She faced her late husband's father, who was a witness in her trial. He brought up the troubled marriage between Kelly and his murdered son as well as her questionable relationship with Greg. While many people tried to argue that Doug Sr. already disliked Kelly, his closeness to the situation proved effective.

Another witness was Laura McDuffie. Laura McDuffie was an inmate who was in jail with Kelly. While the defense pointed out that the convict may not be the most trustworthy source and McDuffie only wanted time off of her sentence, her claims were convincing. McDuffie confessed that Kelly offered her $10,000 to take the fall for the murder of Doug Gissendaner. Kelly went so far as to provide a map and a handwritten statement of what McDuffie should say. A handwriting expert confirmed that the statement was in fact written by Kelly.

Kelly's own friend Pam was a witness for the prosecution, too. Pam told the jury that Kelly called her and told her that she had killed Doug. She called back at a later time and said that Greg had forced her to do it by threatening to kill her and her children. Pam claimed that Kelly said, "I did it,", but the defense claimed that pam heard incorrectly. Other friends also stepped up to voice they're uneasiness with her behavior while her husband was missing.

The strongest witness for the prosecution, though, was Greg Owen. His statement matched very closely with his confession, but there were certain differences that poked holes in his statement. He originally said that he drove for some time and then Kelly arrived when Doug was dead. He changed the time that Kelly showed up to the murder scene as he was finishing murdering Doug. Doug originally stated that he and Kelly burned the car together, but he then changed his story to say that Kelly simply threw a bottle of kerosene out of the window for him and he burned the car alone. Even with some holes in his original story, the confession remained very damning for Kelly. The former lovers found themselves implicating each other in their once common scheme.

The defense stated that the prosecution could not prove Kelly's innocence beyond a reasonable doubt. Furthermore, Doug Gissendaner was significantly larger than Greg and was also trained by the military. It seemed unreasonable that Doug would obey Greg's commands even if he did have a knife. Greg showed no sign of injury or struggle. It also didn't seem fair that Greg only got a life sentence when he was the one who committed the murder. Also, Greg's testimony, which was part of a plea bargain, gave him incentive to implicate Kelly for a lower sentence for himself.

In the end, a trial of her peers found Kelly Gissendaner guilty after deliberating for only two hours and sentenced her to the death penalty. In just a couple of words, Kelly's life came to an end. However, she was going to do whatever she could to save herself.

Life in Prison

Kelly was taken to prison where she was the only woman on death row. Being on death row, Kelly did her best to retain a relationship with her three children. She also continued to appeal her case, focus on her spiritual health, and mentor other prisoners.

While on death row, Kelly could not socialize with the general prison population. However, she could preach and act as a spiritual guide by talking to inmates through a vent. Mrs. Gissendaner created a bit of a name for herself in prison, and the women inmates supported her throughout her trial. They even called themselves the Struggle Sisters and rallied for her to be taken off of death row and allowed to live the rest of her life in prison.

Execution Reschedules

Her actual execution was actually the third time that Gissendaner had been scheduled for execution. She was previously scheduled for execution at the end of February, but the date was changed due to complications with winter weather. Next, she was scheduled for execution in the first week of March, but the doctors at the prison were concerned because the drug used to perform the lethal injection appeared cloudy. They sent a specimen to be tested, and, in April, they announced the results that there was nothing wrong. Gissenander's lawyers tried claiming that the changes in her execution date constituted cruel and unusual treatment, but the case was thrown out. If anything, Kelly was given more time, but her lawyers fought to the end.

Death

It was 12:21 a.m. on a Wednesday morning in Jackson, Georgia when officials declared Kelly MN Gissendaner dead from lethal injection. Her execution was scheduled for 7:00 p.m., but her lawyers attempted to repeal the decision to the very end. One hundred people stood outside of the Georgia Diagnostic and Classification Center in protest of her death. Her last meal was nachos, chips with cheese dip, and frozen lemonade.

Gissendaner showed remorse for her part in her ex-husband's death until the very end. Her last words were, "Bless you all. Tell the Gissendaners I am so, so sorry that an amazing man lost his life because of me. If I could take it all back, I would." Her words can be interpreted to indicate a sense of guilt on Gissendaner's part. It can also be interpreted to indicate a peace with her position.

Kelly Gissendaner was the only woman at death row for the entire duration of her time incarcerated, and she was the first woman to be given the death penalty in Georgia since 1945- over 70 years. She was one of only six women executed in the state, and she was the last woman to be executed in Georgia.

Appeals and Support

Kelly's lawyers made a valiant attempt at an appeal. In fact, the appeal was more than fifty pages when they turned it in, and it had statements from a number of different people, including inmates, the pope, and political figures.

After being approached by Mrs. Gissendaner's lawyer, the pope responded in a letter stating, "While not wishing to minimize the gravity of the crime for which Ms. Gissendaner has been convicted, and while sympathizing with the victims, I nonetheless implore you, in consideration of the reasons that have been presented to your Board, to commute the sentence to one that would better express both justice and mercy."

The endorsement by the pope was powerful, but the Catholic Church had also just recently vocalized a stance against the death penalty. Even former Georgia Supreme Court Chief Justice Norman Fletcher stood up for the defendant saying that her role in the murder did not constitute the death penalty. In addition to these endorsements, 90,000 people also signed a petition to support Kelly. Kelly's lawyers showed the courts that Kelly showed remorse and represented a criminal who had turned her life around to bring positivity to those around her. They argued that her presence was significantly greater than her absence to those around her, especially her children and other inmates.

Mrs. Gissendaner's lawyers attempted three appeals to the U.S. Supreme Court, but they were denied all three times. Unfortunately, on the day of the execution, Mrs. Gissendaner's children had to choose between saying good-bye to their mother or appearing in front of a judge for one last attempt to appeal her case. The last time that they saw their mother was two days earlier on Monday. In the most heartbreaking of all testimonies, Kelly's daughter, Kayla pleaded with the court to save her mother's life. She made the point that she had already lost her dad, and he would not want her or her siblings to endure any further loss by also losing their mother. Despite the emotional appear and strong endorsements, the court did not waver on its original decision.

Despite the support from multiple sources, Douglas's family, especially his father, maintained throughout the trial that they trusted the legal system and agreed with the sentence of the death penalty. They reminded the public that she chose to go to trial instead of pleading guilty. They also reminded the public that Douglas did not get any choice in what happened to his life. After the gruesome death of their son, an exhausting and emotional search for the truth, and a prolonged trial, Douglas Gissendaner Sr. and Sue Gissendaner got justice.

Death Penalty Debate

Kelly Gissendaner's case became famous across the nation because of its legal implications regarding the death penalty. People for the death penalty noted that Kelly had orchestrated the entire murder, she helped dispose of the body, she lied multiple times, and the family of Douglas Gissendaner deserved justice. People opposed to the death penalty noted that there was room for doubt, she technically did not commit the murder, the person who did commit the murder escaped the death penalty, she showed remorse over her part in the murder, she experienced trauma in her childhood, and she regularly preached and encouraged other women in the prison. Men and women all over the country debated the case, but, ultimately, the death penalty ruling was honored by the state of Georgia, and Kelly was executed while she sobbed and sang "Amazing Grace". She was 47-years-old.

WENDI ANDRIANO

Chapter 1

A dying husband needs a devoted wife. But when love runs out, marriage becomes a burden.

On October 8, 2000, Wendi Andriano snapped. She had played the part of devoted wife to her terminally ill husband, Joe Andriano, for years, but when the love left their marriage, so did Wendi's patience for her husband's eventual demise.

Wendi had a plan to help nudge nature along, and when her plan b expired, she took matters directly into her own hands and bludgeoned him to death.

Wendi first tried to poison her husband by spiking his last meal, a homemade beef stew, with sodium azide, but Joe Andriano did not ingest enough to kill him, only enough to vomit it back up. Wendi then grabbed the nearest object, a bar stool, and beat her dying husband over the head so many times that parts of his brain became exposed.

After thinking she had successfully killed her husband twice, Wendi then realized that Joe was still breathing, so she took a knife from the family kitchen and stabbed him in the side of the throat.

Minutes later, Joe was finally dead.

This bizarre and frantic way Wendi killed her husband isn't the strangest thing about the case though. Known even to Wendi, Joe was due to die from terminal cancer within the next few years anyways.

Why Wendi couldn't wait to kill her husband is an intriguing tale wrought with sex, lies, and strangely, a lack of patience.

Chapter 2

Wendi and Joe Andriano grew up together in the small farming community of Casa Grande, Arizona. But while they both had gone to the same school, they never dated. As a minister's daughter, Wendi's social life was restricted to her father's church. Her celebration for graduating high school was even in the form of a missionary trip to

Mexico in 1989. When she returned she took a job at the local clerical hospital.

Wendi met Joe in 1992 through friends. Although when the couple started dating Joe's family found the minister's daughter to be an unusual fit for the loud, outgoing former football player, they all thought she was friendly enough and approved of the match.

Joe worked for a local boat builder. He was very mechanically inclined and was a very good welder. He owned his own boat and took Wendi for several cruises around the local hot spots for speedboats. They were inseparable.

The couple married in January of 1994. Their wedding took place in a baptist church across the street from their shared elementary school. Their reception was at the Elk's club and was populated by their many friends and family. Even after two years of dating, though, Joe's family felt like they didn't know his new bride very well, but Joe seemed to be very happy, so they were happy for him.

Soon after marrying, the couple became business partners when they started a small company that did windshield repair and replacement. The business combined Wendi's office experience with Joe's mechanical experience, skills they both exceeded at, and the business thrived.

The couple hadn't been married a whole year yet before they faced their first major challenge together. That fall, Joe noticed an odd bump on his neck. When he had it tested, he was told it was a non-cancerous benign tumor, but it wasn't long before they were second-guessing the diagnoses. A year after it was removed, the tumor grew back.

A second surgery and round of tests seemed to reconfirm that the tumor was benign, but shortly after Wendi gave birth to a son in 1997, the tumor was back yet again.

The third time the tumor returned, Joe's wife and family were convinced that the tumor had to be cancer. This fear was confirmed in 1998 when Joe underwent surgery to have the bump removed for the fourth time. Joe's pre-surgery chest x-ray showed that not only was the tumor cancerous, but that the cancer had now spread across Joe's throat, chest, and lungs.

The prognosis wasn't good—Joe had a rare form of cancer and while radiation and chemotherapy were standard, there was no guarantee they would work. On top of this, Wendi was also pregnant again and was only months away from giving birth to the couple's second child.

Chapter 3

In an effort to increase Joe's chances of survival while decreasing his suffering, Wendi and Joe decided to pursue holistic treatments before resorting to chemotherapy and radiation. They had been told that chemotherapy and radiation treatments would likely not cure Joe, but they would lengthen his life by a few years; however, these years would be anything from pleasant. The horrific side-effects chemotherapy and radiation treatments cause are well known.

So the Andriano's decided first to try anything from special diets to alternative medical treatments to prayer—anything that had a chance to help Joe. Joe even attended a holistic treatment centre for cancer patients in Colorado for a few weeks where he was surrounded by other men and women facing the same prognosis as him. After seeing the bravery of others in the same position as him, Joe began thinking about his future again and began to see it as bright for the first time in a while.

After Joe returned from his holistic healing getaway with a bright new attitude, the Andriano's decided the next best step would be for Joe to begin chemotherapy treatments. He had begun to crave his future and was ready to take steps to achieve it. Unfortunately, taking these steps meant that Joe needed to quit his welding job as well as his own position in the couple's business.

To help make ends meet, Wendi returned to working for the first time since the birth of the couple's children. She ended up taking multiple jobs and worked long hours while continuing to care for her husband at home. Eventually, Wendi landed a job managing the San Riva apartment complex in the Ahwatukee foothills, an upscale neighbourhood outside of Phoenix.

Wendi's new job came with some major perks—the salary was above average, which was nice as Wendi was now the family's breadwinner, and it required Wendi to live on site, which meant that the family now lived in a luxury apartment but paid no rent. Wendi's new job also gave her a new life. A large part of her duties as complex manager was arranging social activities for the other residents of the San Riva apartments, who were mostly young, wealthy, single businesspeople.

Every Saturday the complex hosted picnics, pool parties, or late-night socials. The residents even had their own baseball team. Wendi was required to attend every event, which meant Joe was needed to stay home with their two children. Wendi enjoyed this alone time so much that many of the residents at the San Riva had no clue she had a dying husband and two children at home. She partied like she was single.

The first few months at the San Riva went well. Wendi organized mixers and pool parties for the tenants while Joe took care of the kids. Despite being very weak from treatments, he did everything he could, he wanted to do it. He preferred to have his kids around him even when he didn't feel good.

Although they had never gotten close to their daughter-in-law, Joe's parents also pitched in with babysitting so the couple could have time alone together. They didn't get to see each other much as Wendi began spending more and more time at work. Her new job had also given her a new confidence, and she spent many nights out on the town dancing and drinking away her weekday stress with friends. Joe began to fear that Wendi would soon leave him for her new lifestyle, but this fear got sidetracked when his health continued to fail.

In the summer of 2000, when tests revealed his cancer had spread yet again, Joe and Wendi decided to increase the frequency of Joe's chemotherapy. Joe agreed to undergo more treatments, but they quickly took their toll. He lost 15 pounds in the first week alone, and Joe's doctor became concerned. It went from bad to worse very quickly.

By the beginning of October 2000, it became harder and harder to remain optimistic about Joe's chances of beating his cancer. It became apparent it was terminal, but doctors insisted that with treatment Joe could live for several more years.

No one had any idea that Joe would be dead after only the first week of the month. No one, that is, except for one person—Wendi Andriano.

Chapter 4

Just after 2:00 a.m. on October 8, Wendi Andriano called a friend who also lived in the San Riva apartment complex. She told her friend that she needed someone to stay with the kids while she took Joe to the hospital. When the friend arrived, she found Joe on the floor, barely alive.

Joe was on the floor in the fetal position. There was vomit on the floor around him and he couldn't stand up. Wendi confided in her friend that she told Joe that she had called 9-1-1 and paramedics were on the way, but this wasn't true. After seeing Joe in such poor condition, the neighbour urged Wendi to call paramedics. She then went outside to wait for them to arrive while Wendi waiting with her husband.

Wendi did call 9-1-1, but when the EMT's arrived minutes later, she refused to let them or her friend inside the apartment. She said that her husband was dying from terminal cancer and had a do not resuscitate order. Joe was not to receive any medical attention.

Just over an hour later, at 3:30 a.m., Wendi dialed 9-1-1 a second time. The same team of paramedics came to the house. It didn't take them long to realize something wasn't quite right, so they contacted the police department. Both the paramedics and the police were shocked to find out that Joe, who had been terminally ill from cancer for quite some time had died, but not from the cancer that had been slowly killing his body. He died from being repeatedly beaten with a bar stool and from being stabbed in the neck.

When the police opened the front door of the apartment, they were confronted with obvious signs of a deadly struggle. The apartment was in a complete state of disarray, and there was blood everywhere. Blood had been traced throughout the kitchen, the dining room, and the living room of the luxury apartment, and blood had spattered across the walls the ceilings. Lying in the middle of the bloody scene was Joe, with a knife wound in his neck and holes spattered across his visible skull.

While crime scene technicians surveyed the apartment, phoenix police took Wendi down to the station for a formal statement. She was wearing clothes drenched in Joe's blood and was armed with a story that explained how Joe's death had been a complete accident.

In the interrogation room, Wendi told police she and joe had spent the evening in Casa Grande visiting with Joe's parents. They put the kids to bed after they returned home, which was when Joe noticed something odd about Wendi's appearance—she wasn't wearing her wedding ring.

According to Wendi, Joe worked himself into a rage and began accusing her of having an affair. This argument turned into a shoving match, and when Joe grabbed a belt, Wendi grabbed a bar stool and swung. Joe went down on all fours so she hit him again. It was then that she called her neighbour for help. Joe may have been in a terrible state when the neighbour saw him, but according to Wendi when she went outside Joe had gotten back to his feet easily.

Wendi said she denied the EMTs access to the apartment because she and Joe were both embarrassed about the fight, but just minutes after the EMTs left, the fight got physical again.

Wendi said that her husband tried to strangle her with a telephone cord and she defended herself with the first weapon she could get in her hands—a kitchen knife. She was vague about how the knife ended up in Joe's neck though, saying she was holding the knife up when Joe suddenly fell flat on his face. The next thing she knew, blood was spurting everywhere. He must have fallen on the blade, it was simply an accident.

Many things about this story didn't make sense to the police. First of all, the timeline presented in Wendi's story didn't match the accounts of Wendi's neighbour or the EMTs. Wendi's neighbour had seen no evidence of a physical fight when they first entered the apartment—there were no broken bar stools or blood like later when the police arrived. As well, Wendi had few injuries on her body, definitely no injuries that would necessitate self defence in the form of murder.

Joe's illness also shed doubt on Wendi's story. Joe's parents told police that when the Andriano's visited earlier that evening, Joe had been so weak from his treatments that he could barely stand. They had spent the evening doting on their sick son, bringing him any comforts he wanted. If he was too weak to stand, he certainly couldn't have been strong enough to violently attack Wendi.

Police also uncovered a damning piece of evidence from Wendi herself, in a moment when she thought she was all alone. The investigators that had been questioning Wendi left her on her own in the interrogation room for some time while they fact checked some of her statements and checked in with the investigators who were scanning the crime scene for evidence. During this time, Wendi made a phone call to a coworker at the apartment complex and asked them to hide some of her files from the police. This immediately led to a search of Wendi's office where police found evidence that Wendi had in fact killed her husband. She had even been planning it for months.

Chapter 5

While both investigators strongly believed that Wendi Andriano was responsible for Joe's death, they were stumped by her motive. Why would Wendi kill her dying husband? The police didn't know, but they did have one intriguing lead—the phone call Wendi had made from the interrogation room. They were determined to find out what she was trying to hide.

When they searched her office, police discovered that Wendi had been disciplined at work for using her computer to search inappropriate items on the internet while on the clock.She had been conducting research on poisons, and how to use certain poisons to kill people. They also discovered the papers that she had tried to hide—shipping notices for a substance known as sodium azide.

Sodium azide is a lethal substance with a variety of industrial uses including propelling airbags. It is not, however, something that the average person can simply go out and buy. It's not restricted to the point where only certain companies can possess it, but it needs to be bought for a reason—something that an apartment complex didn't have. But based on the information on the shipping invoice, Wendi had found a way around that.

Wendi had created a fictitious business license using the tax ID form for the apartment complex. Using a Xerox machine and an exacto knife, Wendi had removed all information specific to the apartment complex and inserted fictitious information for a fake company.

The business name on the shipping notice was bogus, but the address wasn't. Wendi had the substance delivered to an address in Scottsdale, Arizona in an attempt to distance herself, but that plan didn't work. When the police tracked down the real address on the invoice, workers at the company positively identified Wendi as the person who had come by a couple weeks earlier to pick up a package she had mistakenly had shipped there instead of her own office.

Wendi's coworkers had seen her with a package but that she had been very mysterious with the contents. She refused to tell anyone what was inside. Had this been the sodium azide? And if so, where was it now?

Chapter 6

Suspecting that Wendi had tried to poison Joe with the sodium azide, police took samples of every medication and food they could find in the Andriano's apartment. If Joe had ingested poison, it would have explained the awful state Wendi's friend had seen him in just over an hour before he died. Luckily, the remainders of Joe's last supper, homemade beef stew, still sat in a pot on the stove.

However, police didn't find any evidence of Wendi's mysterious package, or any evidence of the sodium azide itself in Wendi and Joe's apartment. They had just begun to lose hope in finding the poison when they found out Wendi had a storage space in the building that she failed to tell the police about. Hidden behind a stack of boxes in Wendi's storage unit was a small bottle of white powder and a measuring spoon. The white powder was soon identified as sodium azide.

But the storage unit wasn't the only place investigators found the lethal substance—it was also in Joe's stomach contents and in the beef stew on the stove.

While discovering the poison helped police understand that Wendi had been trying to kill her husband, it didn't explain why she had bludgeoned him to death on October 8, 2000. Wendi had spent a lot of time researching poisons and she spent a lot of time manufacturing documents so that she could purchase the poison. It certainly wasn't a spur of the moment decision.

But why would Wendi beat and stab her husband if she had already poisoned him? Prosecutors had a theory, one that would cut to the heart of the crime. It was patience—or more precisely, Wendi's lack of it—that had killed Joe in the end.

Wendi had grown tired of waiting for the cancer to kill Joe, so she decided to give nature a little nudge by poisoning his supper. But according to the theory, when Wendi gave Joe the poison, things didn't go quite to plan. Joe hadn't ingested enough poison to kill him when he began vomiting it back up. With her plan quickly failing, Wendi panicked. She snapped.

Now improvising, Wendi beat Joe with the nearest object she could get her hands on—a bar stool. Pathologists were able to conclude that Wendi beat Joe over the head with the stool no less than twenty-four times. This beating did render Joe unconscious, but still didn't kill him so Wendi grabbed a kitchen knife and stabbed him in the part of his body that caused all this trouble in the first place—the side of his neck.

Chapter 7

Ten days after she murdered her husband, Wendi Andriano was formally charged with first degree murder. Wendi's crime was viewed as being especially cruel due to the large amount of suffering Joe had had to endure over several hours thanks to Wendi's actions. Because of this, the prosecutor's on Wendi's trial did the almost unthinkable, they sought the death penalty.

When Wendi a walked into the Arizona courtroom on September 9, 2004 she looked vastly different from the perky apartment manager that the residents of the San Riva apartments used to know.

At the time of the killing she had been blonde, she had short hair, and generally appeared to be much younger and cute than the individual who appeared in court with long dark hair and thick glasses. Previously, she had liked to look good and show her figure so her conservative dress at the trial was certainly different from the look her friends were used to seeing. She was trying to look more conservative, more innocent.

She had had plenty of time to perfect her new look—it had taken prosecutors almost four years to bring the case to trial. It had been postponed about 12 times before it was finally brought before a judge and jury.

In their opening statement, prosecutors reminded the jury that at the time of the murder Wendi had been anything but the perfect mother or wife she claimed to have been. She had been someone who had no disregard for her husband at all. While her husband was dying, she had gone out partying and started affairs, and when his condition worsened, and it began to cramp her style, she turned to poison.

Wendi didn't like her new role as family breadwinner, especially with the loss of Joe's income, and with rising medical bills, the family was in the worst financial state they had ever been in. Wendi had thought she was going to be able to be a stay-at-home-mom for the rest of her life, and she did not adjust well to her return to the workforce. So Wendi had found an out.

Although Joe did not have any life insurance, even though Wendi had asked several friends to pretend to be Joe in medical exams so he could be insured, Joe had filed a malpractice suit against his former doctor who had continually told him his tumor was benign when it was in fact spreading throughout his body. If Joe died and the lawsuit went through, Wendi would likely walk away with a multi-million dollar settlement.

More than money though, Wendi had wanted freedom. She wanted the freedom to be single again, she wanted freedom to the ball-and-chain who was slowly dragging her spirit into his grave along with himself. Wendi wanted to not have to care about her dying husband anymore, who was too weak to provide her with any love.

Wendi maintained her plea of innocence throughout the trial, and her defence team attempted to prove she had been the victim of abuse not only on the night of Joe's death but also throughout the couple's entire marriage. To explain the poison, Wendi told the court that Joe had been the one who had grown tired of waiting for the cancer to end his life, and had asked Wendi to help him do it himself.

On the witness stand Wendi said that Joe had willingly taken the poison, but she also stuck by the story that she had originally told police, that Joe had suspected an affair and became enraged when she affirmed them. He became deranged and attacked her, starting the bloody fight. Wendi claimed Joe had died during the ensuing struggle.

Wendi's story wasn't enough to convince the court though, and on November 18, 2004 she was found guilty of the crime. It had taken the jury only two-and-a-half-hours to come to its unanimous decision. Six years after her husband joe had been diagnosed with terminal cancer, Wendi Andriano faced a possible death sentence of her own.

On December 20, 2004, the jurors assigned to Wendi Andriano's case met and decided on Wendi's fate—it would be death for Ms Andriano. Wendi, along with most of the courtroom, was aghast. Even Joe's family was shocked by the decision. Wendi Andriano became the second ever woman to be put on death row in Arizona, a state that reserves the death penalty for the worst of the worst.

Wendi Andriano has since attempted to appeal the court's decision, but as of early 2017, all attempts have been denied and Wendi continues to wait on death row. Wendi and Joe's children now live with Joe's parents, who continue to mourn the loss of their beloved son.

Joe Andriano's death was especially long, and especially cruel, but no happy ending was found when Wendi was sentenced to her own death. Many view the conclusion of this case to be the saddest possible outcome. On October 8, 2000, two lives were lost, and two children were left without parents.

HUSBAND KILLER : THE TRUE STORY OF LARISSA SCHUSTER

65

ERIN EDWARDS

Larissa Leann Foreman was born January 1, 1960. She grew up on a farm near Clarence Missouri. By all accounts she had a happy childhood. She won first place at the Randolph pony show, her father, Charles, won first place in the men's division and Deeann, her mom, won second in the bareback for pleasure division. Her parents seemed to be very involved in her life. She excelled academically; she was athletic and went after what she wanted with everything she had. She was described as a 'go getter'.

Larissa graduated High school and went on to the University of Missouri Columbia to become a biochemist. She didn't come from a rich family so she would work as a nursing aide at Boone Hospital Center in Columbia Missouri. It's not known whether she liked her work as an aide, however she did like a nurse named Tim Schuster, and he liked her as well. She was electrifying and intoxicating, Tim was enthralled. They started dating after becoming friends and just hanging out together after work.

Finally, in 1982 Tim popped the question, and Larissa said yes. Between 1982 and the birth of their second child Tyler in 1990 there was a whirlwind of things happening. There was the wedding in '82, the birth of their first child, Kristin, and a move to sunny central California, Fresno to be exact.

In the beginning Tim managed the cardiology Department for St Agnes Medical Center. While Larissa worked for Pan Agricultural Laboratories. Larissa saw the company declining and thought it a good time to start her own company; Central California Research Lab. She was ambitious and worked long hours to make her company a success. Tim continued to work at St Agnes and be both Mom and Dad to their two children.

According to friends Bob and Mary Solis, Tim was the one who made sure doctor appointments were kept, homework was done and dinner was cooked and on the table. Larissa ruled her house and Tim having a non-confrontational personality went along with her, if for no other reason than to keep the peace. By this time she was making more than twice what Tim made. It was her money that made it possible for them to move to Clovis and buy a much larger home than the one they had in Fresno. It looked like they had it all...but did they?

By this time Kristen was a teenager and as with most teens there was attitude. Kristen fought with her mother at almost every turn. She stood up to Larissa in such a way that she felt she had no other option than to send her daughter to her parents in Clarence, Missouri. Tim was upset that his wife didn't even discuss this move with him; she'd decided this IS what will happen. And soon his beloved little girl was gone. But still Tim kept quiet.

The Schuster's entered into a bitter, rancorous separation in 2002, after nearly 20 years of marriage and two children. They tried living in the same house after the separation. However Larissa was not happy with this arrangement. From the very beginning she didn't want Tim to have anything to do with Tyler, no visitation and no kind of a relationship with his son at all. This was not okay with Tim. On more than one occasion she made the statement that she wished Tim would just die.

In late June or early July Larissa took Tyler and went on a trip out of state. Tim took this opportunity to secure a condo and move out of the family's home. Larissa was livid that he would have the nerve to leave while she was away and accused him of taking things from the house that didn't belong to him. What earlier seemed like idle threats became something more, she told a neighbor that she should just get it over with and kill Tim herself.

A Plan started formulating shortly after Tim moved out of the Clovis family home. Larissa asked James Fagone a lab assistant and Larissa's sometimes babysitter, sometimes whipping boy if he would help break in to Tim's house and help her get back somethings he took when he moved out. She felt he wasn't entitled to them and left messages on his answering machine telling him he'd better bring them back...or else.

After returning from a trip Tim came home to a house that had been burglarized and ransacked. One of the things missing...the very set of mixing bowls Larissa had had such a fit over. Who was her accomplice in the break-in...none other than James Fagone? Larissa wasn't shy about what they had done, she told her manicurist Terri Lopez, that after the break-in she would go back to Tim's house and sit in a chair and look around at what they had done. She also told Tami Belshay that "it gave her a feeling that was better than sex."

After the burglary the Schuster's relationship went even further downhill. Tim knew who had broken into his condo. Larissa's bitterness not only let her destroy things in the condo, but she even bragged about keying his truck. She said it made her happy every time she saw the marks on his truck. Tim seemed worried about what his estranged wife was capable of. He moved again, this time to a house in Clovis that had motion sensors and an alarm. He obtained a handgun and a permit to carry a concealed weapon. Larissa had told her manicurist Ms. Lopez that she prayed every night that Tim would just die. At one point Larissa told her that she could kill Tim and get away with it. She also asked one of the employees at CCRL if her boyfriend knew anyone that would kill Tim or at least rough him up. She'd made remarks like this before and all who heard them thought she was just venting because the divorce wasn't going the way she wanted it to. She said she would do anything to keep Tim from getting the business.

According to Bob and Mary Solis, Larissa would belittle and embarrass Tim in front friends and family alike. She seemed to relish the power she had over him.

In late June St Agnes let everyone know that there would be a round of layoffs coming and to be expecting it. Tim and his friend Mary Solis was on the short list to be let go. Larissa laughed when she heard the news. On July 9th Tim, Mary, her husband Bob and another friend Victor Uribe all had dinner together. The group broke up about 10pm that night, before Tim left the Solis' they had made arrangements to meet for breakfast the next morning. Tim never showed for his exit meeting or for breakfast. This worried Bob and Mary, it seems Tim was never late for anything, and if he thought he was going to be late he called. He was also supposed to pick up Tyler that evening.

His friends tried to reach Tim, calling his cell phone. Finally they called Uribe and told him that they couldn't reach Tim and would he go by the house and check on their friend. Uribe arrived at Tim's house and went inside. There didn't seem to be anything out of place, until he went to the bedroom. Tim's watch, wallet and cell phone were lying on the dresser. Uribe was now worried as well. Victor said "He never went anywhere without his cell, he kept it with him at all times, in case the kids needed him."

No one knew what had happened to Tim. The police refused to even take a missing person's report until he'd been missing 24 hours. July 10th when Tim had not been heard from in the allotted time Bob Solis filed the missing person's report. Officer John Willow from the Clovis Police Department responded to the call.

Willow found Tim's handgun under a cushion of a chair. He found Tim's cell phone in the bedroom and called all the numbers in his contacts to see if any of them had seen or heard from Mr. Schuster. When he called Larissa she said she hadn't heard from him either. He also talked to Terri Lopez and she relayed to Willow that the Schuster's were going through a rather nasty divorce. John Willow decided to turn the case over to Detectives Larry Kirkhart and Vincent Weibert.

When they entered Tim's home they noted some damage on the wall behind the chair where the gun was found earlier. They found a briefcase in the same room as the chair. Inside they found a microcassette recorder and tape. In the bedroom they found an answering machine that showed only one number, a cell phone number belonging to Larissa Schuster. Detective Kirkhart then asked Larissa to come to the police station for a chat about her missing husband.

During her interview with the detectives she told them that she and Tim were getting a divorce and that they did not communicate very well with each other. They asked her about her cell number being on the caller ID. She fabricated a story about being asleep on her couch and waking up to find she had pushed some buttons and maybe she had speed dialed Tim. They asked her if she had her phone with her and she said no. Kirkhart called for a pause in the interview and went to the parking lot to find Larissa's car. He looked in the window and saw a phone on the center console, dialed her number and the phone in the car rang.

Kirkhart went back to the interview room and asked Larissa to come with them to unlock her car and retrieve her phone. Back inside the station the interview resumed. The detective went through her contacts that she had on speed dial, none of them were Tim's number.

Larissa's whole demeanor changed, she was shaking and in the opinion of the detectives showing signs of deceit. She came clean and admitted that she had lied to the detectives and she knew she shouldn't have. She claimed she wasn't trying to be deceitful. None the less they let Schuster go home, for now. At this point in their investigation they still had no idea what had happened to Tim. Kirkhart had asked Larissa if she thought that Tim could just cash out some money and leave town, go camping or to Vegas to just get away. She told them she didn't think he would do that, that he wouldn't leave his son like that. This was still just a missing person case and most of Tim's friends thought that perhaps he had just had enough, the divorce, the custody battle, losing his job was to much for him to handle. Tami Belshay, Bob and Mary Solis and Victor Uribe were among those friends. The detectives were thinking the same thing at this point.

With no solid leads on Tim's whereabouts detectives Weibert and Kirkhart kept searching for some clue, however small that might give them some direction on finding Tim. Kirkhart was going through Tim's ledger provided to them by Larissa. And they came across a name they were familiar with...James Fagone. They knew his name because he was the one suspected of breaking into Tim's house with Larissa shortly after Tim moved out of the family home a year earlier. They also knew that he was an associate of sorts of Larissa's.

The following Monday Detectives Kirkhart and Daly called Fagone to come and talk with them. Vince Weibert thought that perhaps Fagone might have some "inside" information on Tim's disappearance.

It seems that Fagone was a babysitter for the Schuster's son Tyler, before and after their separation. James was a good kid according to his attorney Peter Jones. "He's an above average student, higher than a 4.0 grade point average...a gentle spirit."

Fagone was nervous during the police interview. He admitted that Larissa had him help her break into Tim's house and take back things that she didn't want him to have.

James told the detectives that Larissa was going around the house looking for things and he just wanted to get the TV and some other stuff so he wasn't paying attention to what she was doing. Obviously James was scared out of his mind by now, but they pressed him more telling him they "knew he was involved somehow" with Tim's disappearance. Fagone's determination not to tell what had happened, what him and Larissa Schuster had done crumbled.

Fagone confessed that he had been there the night that Tim went missing, that he had gone to his house with a weapon. James relayed to them that Larissa had paid him the $2000 to purchase a stun gun and that he could just keep the rest for himself.

So as the day wore on James conveyed the sordid details of the night in questions.

On the night that Tim lost his job at St Agnes and had dinner with a group of friends, James had done what he was told to do by

Larissa, buy a stun gun. Later he would get the call from her (Larissa). She picked him up and went to Tim's house. James laid in wait in the darkness just outside of his door. He could hear Larissa on the phone telling Tim that Tyler wasn't feeling well and she needed him to come to the front door.

A few moments later Tim opened the front door and James sprung from the shadows and attacked him wrestling him to the ground. Tim was struggling; James was using the stun gun on him, on the arm at first, not sure where else he might have zapped him. Soon Tim stopped struggling and when James looked up he saw Larissa with a rag that had been soaked in chloroform.

Were the detectives hearing this right? Was Fagone confessing to the murder of Timothy Schuster? But if they were going to believe any of it they needed some kind of evidence. They asked about the stun gun again, and what had Fagone done with it. He told them he threw it in a portable toilet on the edge of town. The investigators found the stun gun, right where James told them it should be.

Now at the same time Fagone was being interviewed Clovis Police Department got a call from a woman saying that her boss ask her to do something that in retrospect seemed a little off, suspicious even. Her Boss...Larissa Schuster. Leslie Dodd had been instructed to rent a moving truck by her boss. She was told to use her personal credit card and rent it in her own name not her boss's. A year earlier Larissa had asked the same employee to rent a storage unit near Schuster's lab, again to do it in the employees name and with her personal credit card.

Jim Koch got the call to check it out. He went to the storage unit and walked down the hall. He had been told to look for a blue barrel. When he found Schuster's unit and opened the door "there was a very very strong odor." Koch said. "I had on a breathing apparatus and gloves."

He saw the blue barrel, he opened it.

Koch said in an interview, "And when I opened the barrel I—I saw something that was very, very shocking to me and I recognized immediately as human remains. There was a barrel that's over 3/4 of the way full of fluid and portions of—of—body protruding from the fluid. And the body was obviously decaying. It was placed in acid. And the acid was basically eating away at the body."

Had Larissa Schuster killed her husband and put him in the barrel? According to James Fagone, yes she had, and he had helped her and then watched as she poured a caustic solution in on top of Tim. Worst of all, Tim was probably still alive when the acid was poured on him and he was sealed inside the barrel.

Tim had been found, the truth had come out and the Clovis detectives were on their way to Missouri to arrest Larissa for the murder of her husband Tim. They met her at the airport where she had gone to see her family. According to the detectives that arrested her for the murder she didn't even ask what had happened to Tim or how he died.

Both James Fagone and Larissa Schuster were arrested and charged with 1st degree murder.

Now that the perpetrators of Tim Schuster's murder had been arrested it was time to take them to trial. The murder was committed in the early morning hours of July 10, 2003. There was a lot left to do before the trial could begin.

The Clovis police department had to finish gathering evidence, talk to friends and family to make sure that everything was done correctly. They wanted to make sure that Larissa and James would not be let go on a technicality.

The judge had to decide if he would make this a death penalty case or a life in prison without parole case. That would be decided later. The prosecutor had to prepare a rock solid case and present the evidence to a jury in a manner that would guarantee a conviction. The defense would also be talking to people on behalf of their clients. Find people that had nothing but good things to say about them in hopes of offsetting the horrible truths that would come out at trial.

The judge separated the cases and James and Larissa would be tried separately. James was tried first. His attorney portrayed James as a misguided man who hero worshipped Larissa.

He was found guilty and is now serving a life without parole sentence.

There was so much media coverage on Larissa that the defense asked and received a change of venue. Her trial was moved to Los Angeles.

Monday October 22, 2007 Larissa's trial started. Prosecutor Dennis Peterson relayed to the jury of 9 women and 3 men just how the murder went down. He told them that Tim was still alive when the acid was poured over him while he laid head first inside the blue barrel. Her motive? She didn't want to share anything that they built during their 19 ½ years of marriage. She felt Tim didn't deserve any part of the business, or home and didn't want him to have contact with their tween son, Tyler.

CCRL employees would also testify to the facts of the blue barrel being at the lab and the day Tim was reported missing went to look for it and it was gone. They also said that Larissa had said that she should just shove Tim in the barrel and get rid of him.

A large amount of Hydrochloric acid, 12 gallons and Sulfuric acid, 4 gallons was ordered for Schuster's lab, more than ever before. Leslie Dodd (nee Fichera) testified that, "that was more acid than the lab would use in a year."

Joseph Boatwright thought Larissa was joking when she asked "if he thought a body would fit in the blue barrel."

Juror's watched several hours of Larissa's police interview. She made Tim out to be controlling and having a volatile temper. After seeing that part of the interview Bob Solis testified to the contrary, that Tim was very calm and a non-violent, non-confrontational person.

In another part of the interview with Clovis Detectives Schuster stated that "she prayed that Tim would get over this hostility about the divorce." Her manicurist Terri Lopez told a different story. Lopez said that "she told me she prayed every night he would die."

A hair stylist Becky Holland sometimes did Larissa's hair. During those appointments Larissa would rant about Tim. Holland didn't think much about it because she knew they were going through a divorce. Later though she said the hateful remarks escalated, Holland told the court, "this is getting a little creepy. It was so intense."

The jurors got to hear just how intense it was when they got to hear message after message of Larissa calling her husband awful names and making threats about their children. The prosecutor used these recordings to make a point to the jury; Larissa was in a "murderous rage". Nuttall interjected that these messages were left on Tim's machine 7 months before the murder.

And with this the prosecution rested, hoping that they had proved their case. There was one witness that they really needed to be able to lockdown the case against Schuster, they needed James Fagone. The judge had barred his confession so the jury would never hear in his own words what happened July 10, 2003. But he refused to cooperate with Peterson because he had already filed his appeal. The only thing that might have helped Peterson is the fact that James Fagone had already been convicted of Tim's murder.

Nuttall began the defense's case by telling the jury that neither he nor his client could tell them what had happened to Tim because "we don't know". And since the jury heard nearly nothing about Fagone, Roger Nuttall blamed the murder on him. After all Fagone had already been found guilty of the murder Larissa was now on trial for. Nuttall said in his opening statements that "Tim was an angry man who belittled Larissa in over-compensation for his own failings as a husband and father." And that "he began stalking Larissa after the divorce proceedings started."

Now Defense attorney Nuttall brought in a stream of witnesses that would steer the blame away from his client.

He had a medical expert that said the victim's body was cut in half and that the police had completely missed a second crime scene and the evidence from there would have proved that Fagone and others were responsible for Tim's murder not Larissa.

Nuttall even had psychiatrist Stephen Estner on the stand. Estner said that, "My impression was that Mrs. Schuster was a very direct and assertive person, and Mr. Schuster was a more passive and nurturing personality. And I think they started butting heads over that."

Larissa Schuster took the stand in her own defense and adamantly denied the charges saying, "No, I did not kill my husband." Again James Fagone would have the whole murder put squarely on him. Schuster told the jury, ""I heard him say something like 'there had been an accident and Tim is dead.' I thought he was joking."

She said that the $2000 payment to Fagone was for babysitting Tyler and housesitting while she was away on vacation with her son. Schuster said the large amount of acid was for cleaning a large scale of lab glass. Schuster seemed to explain everything away poking holes in the prosecutor's case. Would it be enough to get an acquittal? Had she actually swayed the jury?

It seemed that the trial was plagued with problems, including accusations of juror misconduct. At least one juror was replaced by an alternate due to disruptive behavior. Another admonished for giving Larissa a 'thumbs up' after her testimony. And yet with all of that...it was time for the jury to deliberate of the weeks of testimony they'd heard.

It took a little more than two days for the jury to decide on a verdict.

Guilty of Murder with a special circumstance of financial gain. The verdict came exactly one year after Fagone's.

Roger Nuttall slowed the sentencing of Larissa Schuster while he tried to find reasons to ask for a new trial. He even used the argument that there may have been juror misconduct. Nuttall wanted to talk to the jurors but Ellison said no. Nuttall appealed and the District court of Appeals told Ellison to contact the jurors on Schuster's behalf. All the jurors and alternates refused to speak to her attorney.

So on May 8, 2008, five months after being found guilty of her estranged husband's murder Larissa Leeann Schuster was sentenced to life in prison without the possibility of parole. Judge Ellison also denied her request for a new trial.

At the sentencing a total of seven people stood up to make statements about how they had been affected by the murder of Timothy Allen Schuster.

Kristen, Tim and Larissa's oldest child and only daughter made an emotionally charged statement to and about her mother.

She called her mother a demon for "taking my father away." And told her. "I pray you're continually haunted at night by the sight and sound of my father fighting for his last breathing moments on this earth. I hope you toss and turn and have horrible nightmares visualizing the horrific act of violence you have committed. Maybe later in life I can learn to forgive you, but I doubt it. This is goodbye, not just for now, but forever. This is goodbye as your daughter."

Kristen was so devastated over her father's murder she reached out to a support group murdervictims.com. Several people shared their own experiences of losing a parent at a young age hoping she could find at least a little peace.

ALICIA SHAYNE LOVERA

The life of Alicia Shayne Lovera looked like something out of a soap opera.

Born into poverty, she was ushered into a life of wealth and privilege when her mother married a rich president of a bank. She grew up to be beautiful, popular and spoiled. But she soon find herself in financial ruin when her stepfather committed suicide, leaving the family with nothing.

Her sense of entitlement still intact, she married a struggling math teacher who couldn't resist her charms.

But when the marriage became an inconvenience, she did what all black widows do.

She killed her husband.

This is her story.

EARLY LIFE

Alicia Shayne Good was born in 1966 to teenage parents. Going by her middle name Shayne, her early life wasn't easy as her parents lacked the necessary resources to provide. Her mother would divorce her father. But when Shayne turned seven-years old things to a turn for the better.

"Her mother and she were poor," journalist Jamie Satterfield said. "Her mother met Brent Mills who was a bank president and they married into that family and Brent adopted Shayne."

The change in life circumstance was jarring to the young Shayne. She was instantly given an upgrade in lifestyle as she the world was now her oyster. There were expensive vacations, cars and garish parties.

Her new stepfather, Brent Mills, was a bank executive who treated Alicia and her mother Sandy to all the spoils his job could bring. He was well regarded in the business community and had several contacts.

But Brent had inherited the bank built by his father and lacked his business acumen. He was lenient in granting loans and the bank soon grew insolvent. He was also suspected of using the bank as a money laundering service for drug dealers.

On the surface, Brent told the family that the allegations were all fraudulent. He gave them every assurance that everything would be okay.

Then he killed himself.

"He took a gun to his head and blew his brains out," forensic psychologist Paula Orange said. "That left an indelible image on Shayne's outlook on life."

His suicide would leave the family in financial ruin. The papers would ridicule Mills, giving voice to all of the wild allegations of his mismanagement. The family would be left shamed and with nothing.

The effect was devastating on Shayne. She would go from being the richest girl in the school to being dirt poor.

Again.

Shayne just wanted to get away. She had entertained aspirations of being broadcast anchor, thinking that her beauty and speaking skills would lead to an easy gig. So she decided to move out of state for college. She would attend a university in Missouri where she would meet Kelly Lovera.

They would marry a year later.

The couple would have two children over the next five years despite being the polar opposites temperamentally.

Kelly was cool, calm and wanted a quiet life. He didn't embrace the partying lifestyle that Shayne wanted.

"Theirs was a union that is hard to comprehend," Orange said. "Kelly was not en route to becoming the next bank president. He was a twenty-year old student who was struggling. He wanted to be a math teacher. Shayne wanted to live a hedonistic lifestyle. She wanted to party and spend lavishly. Why they would get married defies explanation."

Bored in Missouri, Shayne would then convince Kelly to move back to her hometown in Tennessee. Kelly would consent to the move.

A RETURN TO POVERTY

The couple would live in Sevierville which was thirteen miles north of her former luxury home in Gatlinburg. But it was light years away in terms of affluence as they were forced to rent out a small, one story townhouse.

The neighborhood they lived in was called "Frog Alley".

"A luxury once experienced becomes a necessity," Orange said. "Shayne had gotten used to living the high life. But married life, particularly one with of a lack of resources, would prove to be difficult for her."

"Frog Alley was a place for the working poor," Satterfield said. "To come back and live there would be extremely embarrassing for her."

Kelly's focus was not on making money. He was working on his master's degree in mathematics while he took a teaching position at Pellissippi College in Knoxville. Shayne would work various odd jobs to help the family make ends meet and was not happy about that.

"She had wild ambitions to become a news anchor," Orange said. "But she didn't do anything to make that happen. She wanted someone else to do all the work for her just like she experienced when her step-father financed her life."

BOREDOM SETS IN

Shayne entertained neighbors for barbecues and poker nights. The problem is, the only people that seemed to come around were other men.

She was thoroughly bored with her marriage and began to have multiple affairs.

"She would flirt with men in full view of the children," Orange said. "Men would come over ostensibly to play cards. She would play 'footsie' with them underneath the poker table. She didn't want to be a mother and got bored with that act. She wanted to party, to be the rich wild girl that she was as a teenager. The idea of staying home with a boring math teacher and two needy children was anathema to her. She wanted a way out."

The affairs would occur in her apartment when Kelly was away. Different men would come and go at various hours.

"He's (Kelly) cramping my style," Shayne told one of her lovers. "And you're so much better than him."

"Thanks," her lover said with a grin.

"Do you know anything about how to poison someone?"

"Excuse me?"

"You know," Shayne said. "How certain poisons are undetectable."

Shayne would test the waters with her lovers. She would ask them about poisons in a joking manner. But then they would soon realize that she was serious. There was an ulterior motive to her affairs.

She wanted to find someone to kill her husband.

And she would find a willing assassin in Brett Rae.

THE NEXT DOOR NEIGHBOR

Brett was young and inexperienced with women. He had never encountered anyone like the sexy Shayne Lovera.

"Brett fell very hard for Shayne," Satterfield said. "Their affair started very quickly. And it was hot and heavy."

"Brett was a rich kid," Satterfield said. "His father was a newspaper publisher (Rick Rae, a Canadian publisher of the Sevier County newspaper). He was a well-to-do guy. He was just wild. He was just one of those people who was 'full-on' all of the time. He was up for anything."

And he was completely infatuated with Shayne.

Shayne set up Brett the same way she set up her other lovers. After a torrid session of lovemaking, she popped the question.

Will you kill my husband?

"I'll do anything for you," he told her with baited breath.

Shayne offered him a deal.

"If he were to get rid of Kelly," Satterfield said. "Then he would get her. That's what Brett wanted."

"Brett let his little head do the thinking for his big head," Orange said. "He was going to inherit money from his father so he had absolutely nothing to gain by killing Shayne's husband. Nothing except sex which of course if he had money, he would have more options than a narcissistic married woman. He simply did not have the life experience to see Shayne for what she was."

She would have a party on November 5th, 1994, an outdoor barbecue with gambling and drinking. Kelly left the party early and went to sleep on the couch.

Brett would be the last one to leave that evening. On his way out the door, they both noticed Kelly asleep on the couch.

"It was a spontaneous thing," Orange said. "They didn't have a murder weapon so they used whatever was immediately available. That would be the baseball bat of Kelly's son."

Kelly would then be bludgeoned to death.

"The plan was to put him in his own vehicle," Satterfield said. "And make it look like an accident."

Brett then dragged Kelly into his jeep and drove down Highway 14. He parked near an embankment and pushed the jeep down the side, watching it carom into a tree.

He then called one of his friends to pick him up.

Brett did not keep the news of the murder to himself. He would brag to two of his friends of what he had done.

"I put him (Kelly) over a hundred foot embankment," Brett said. "I fucked his wife and killed his ass. She told me I'd get more sex and more money if I get rid of him so I did."

Brett told his friends of the other methods he thought of using to kill Kelly but that he decided to beat him to death with the baseball bat then "stage a car crash."

FINDING THE BODY

A pair of tourists would discover Kelly's black jeep below the road. Inside, they would see his bloodied dead body. Initially, they believed that he was the victim of an accident. They called the authorities and reported that it appeared as if his jeep had gone off the road and hit a tree

Park Ranger Jerry Grubb was notified of the "accident" at the Great Smoky Mountains National Park.

The whole scene, however, looked suspicious from the get-go.

"Just wasn't any skid marks," Grubb said. "No disturbed gravel. There just wasn't any disturbance in that area."

Grubb looked inside the jeep and found the body of Kelly Lovera, laying in a pool of blood trailing toward the front seat. The blood should have been trailing behind the victim if he had, in fact, struck the tree head on.

Additionally, Kelly's injuries were not consistent with a car crash victim. The facial injuries appeared to be the result of a beating, not the impact of the jeep against the tree.

MURDER ON THEIR HANDS

The autopsy would reveal that Kelly had been beaten to death and a homicide investigation ensued. Authorities would then visit Shayne's apartment and inform her of her husband's death.

She would go into hysterics, sobbing uncontrollably.

"Do you know why anyone would want to do this to him?" an investigator asked.

"He doesn't have any enemies!" she bawled.

But an officer would notice blood splatter on the glass of Kelly's diploma that was placed on a wall near the couch. They would obtain a search warrant and a crime team would arrive, spraying luminol over the apartment.

Luminol lightens up blood stains when a fluorescent ray is scanned over it.

"The whole living room lit up like a Christmas tree," Orange said. "That is when they knew they had the guilty party."

Detectives then began to question neighbors who all pointed their fingers at Brett Rae, the lover of Shayne.

Both Shayne and Brett were arrested and charged with first-degree premeditated murder.

Brett would confess quickly. He admitted to using the baseball bat and then staging the car wreck. He would be represented by Robert Ritchie who would prep him for the murder trial for nearly three months. Ritchie, however, would notice that Brett was completely obsessed with Shayne. He then turned the case over to Robert Ogle but two weeks before the trial Alan Feltes was brought in as Brett was given joint representation.

"His attorneys were flabbergasted at his refusal to give up Shayne," Orange said. "He was truly in love with her and wanted to protect her even if it meant incriminating himself."

"I did it," Brett insisted. "Just leave her out of it."

Feltes told Brett that there was no way he could win the case with all of the evidence stacked against him. The only thing Brett cared about was putting Shayne in jeopardy.

THE TRIAL

Park Ranger Jerry Grubb would testify against the killing duo, presenting the forensic evidence found at the home and jeep. Friends and family would testify that both Shayne and Brett had bragged to them about what they had done.

Going in desperation mode, Shayne would then take the stand. She wanted to tell her version of what happened that night.

"Brett had stopped by to talk to me when Kelly came out and confronted him," Shayne said. "They began fighting and Brett picked up a baseball bat. He swung it only to keep Kelly away. But then he accidentally hit him and killed him."

Shayne would go on to say that she didn't witness any of this. She was asleep and really knew nothing that happened.

"Brett and I were not lovers," Shayne said. "We were nothing more than neighbors. It was a case of fatal attraction. He had a thing for me and wanted to kill my husband."

She didn't know, however, that when both she and Brett were released on bail they were followed by a Siever County Sheriff. He followed them into the mountains and saw them having intercourse in the woods.

When Shayne was confronted with this evidence, she tried to regroup.

"I had sex with Brett," Shayne said. "But only because I had to. He threatened to involve me in the murder plot. My purpose in going there was trying to save what little bit of life I had left at that point."

The explanation did not go over well with the jury. It took them only an hour and a half to return with a guilty verdict.

OFF TO JAIL

On January 29th, 1996, both Shayne and Brett would be convicted of Kelly's murder. They would not be given the death penalty, however. The prosecution wanted a sentence of life without parole.

Feltes approached by the attorneys for Shayne. They stated that a plea agreement would be possible but it would have to be a package deal with Brett.

Feltes advised Brett to take the deal as the plea agreement would guarantee him a life sentence with possibility of parole. If he didn't take the deal, the odds would be that he would be facing life without parole.

"Just don't do anything to hurt Shayne," Brett said. "I want to see her."

"What?"

"I want to see her before I take the deal."

Brett would persist in wanting to see Shayne. Instead he would take the deal.

"His attorneys described him as having the saddest eyes they had ever seen in a courtroom," Orange said. "He was truly in love with Shayne. She, on the other hand, threw him under the bus. She was willing to say whatever it took to get herself off and it backfired."

THE AFTERMATH

Kelly's children would be placed into the care of his parents. Brett and Shayne would receive life with parole after twenty-five years.

Brett would later try to appeal his sentencing despite agreeing to a plea bargain which barred him from doing so.

His claim would be rejected.

Ray would write that "his trial was ineffective for encouraging him to accept the state's offer of life with possibility of parole; failing to prepare for mitigating circumstances at the sentencing phase; failing to properly conduct a pre-trial investigation; failing to adequately consult with him during critical stages of the proceedings; failing to advise him of his rights to direct appeal and collateral attack of his conviction; deficient performance of counsel at trial; his guilty plea was coerced and involuntary; and his conviction is void as violating the protection against double jeopardy."

"He had conceded his guilt during the guilty plea hearing and that his attorneys did the best they could...he made these admissions only because the attorneys instructed him to do so and although he agreed that he believed himself to be guilty of first degree murder at the time of his plea, he now retracts that admission."

Brett's attorney Feltes would dispute his allegations, stating that he "never had any problem with Brett being incoherent or not understanding anything he was told or advised."

Both Brett and Shayne remain in prison, waiting to be paroled in 2025.